History & Guide

POULTON-LE-FYLDE

Christine Storey

TEMPUS

First published in 2001
Copyright in this edition © Christine Storey, 2001

Tempus Publishing Limited
The Mill, Brimscombe Port,
Stroud, Gloucestershire, GL5 2QG

ISBN 0 7524 2442 4

Typesetting and origination by
Tempus Publishing Limited
Printed in Great Britain by
Midway Colour Print, Wiltshire

*I dedicate this book to the memory of Thomas Lewtas (1842-1914),
a master joiner of Poulton and my great-grandfather.*

08734522

Bibliography

The History of Blackpool and its Neighbourhood (1837), William Thornber.
History of the Fylde of Lancashire (1876), John Porter.
History of the Parish of Poulton-le-Fylde (1885), Henry Fishwick.
Lancashire Victoria County History, (1902).
The Archaeology of Lancashire (1996) Lancaster University Archaeological Unit.
General View of the Agriculture of the County of Lancaster (1795), John Holt.
A History of Baines Grammar School (1928), Arthur Pagett.
The Origins of Lancashire (1991), Denise Kenyon.
St Chad's Parish Records, Lancashire Record Office.
The Beginning of Poulton Methodism, Norman Cunliffe.
Valerie Oldham – unpublished dissertation.

CONTENTS

INTRODUCTION & ACKNOWLEDGEMENTS

The history of Poulton is as much about the history of the people who have lived here as anything else. This book sets out to investigate oral and documentary evidence to gain an insight into Poulton's past. The writer trusts that readers will understand that limitations of space mean that it will be impossible to include information on everything and everywhere in this story.

Particular thanks are due to Dr Alan Crosby for his interest and support of Poulton-le-Fylde Historical and Civic Society over many years; to Ben Edwards, former Lancashire County Archaeologist; to Ted Lightbown, Norman Cunliffe and Margaret Panikkar for discussions on local history matters and to Richard Watson for discussions regarding the church style and other matters of local interest. Thanks also to the staff of the Lancashire Record Office and of the Lancashire Archaeological Unit and the Committee of the Society.

Finally my special thanks to Alan, Andrew and Stephen for their interest and support.

I would like to acknowledge:
Lancashire Record Office for copies of tithe maps and the seventeenth-century road map; the Environment Directorate of Lancashire County Council for the aerial photograph of Shard Bridge; Harris Museum Preston for the photograph of the elk. The majority of the old photographs included in the book have been provided by members and friends of the Society and residents of Poulton. Modern photographs were taken by the author.

CHAPTER 1

Before Poulton

One Friday evening in July 1970 a householder living in an area known as High Furlong took a look into a trench on a piece of spare land adjoining his garden where builders had been using a JCB to prepare footings for new houses. He was surprised to see what looked like a large bone embedded in the ground close to the hedge on the boundary between his property and the building site. This chance find was to be of international significance. The resulting archaeological dig found an almost complete skeleton of an elk that was subsequently dated to be around twelve thousand years old. Particular significance lay in the injuries to the bones and barbed tips which lay close by, one embedded in a hind leg just above the hoof. Evidence showed that this site had once been the edge of a lake, surrounded by trees and shrubs. Probably the incident had occurred in winter when the lake was iced over. The animal had been hunted and probably severely injured, escaped onto the ice-covered lake but eventually drowned. Seventeen wounds discovered on the animal had been caused by a variety of weapons, indicating perhaps the hunters' desperate but unsuccessful efforts to recover the carcase for food. Unsuccessful, because the skeleton is almost intact and is now on display in the Harris Museum, Preston. This chance discovery provides the earliest evidence of man in the North West. At this time Britain was part of the mainland of Europe and the area which was to become Poulton

Excavation of the elk in the summer of 1970.

12,000 years later lay far from the sea. Evidence of the woodland which covered this part of Lancashire in prehistoric times is still visible in the present peat beds, with great trunks and roots of oak, yew, silver birch and hazel still finding their way to the surface.

Our knowledge of the prehistory of the area and of the wandering tribes who lived as hunter-gatherers between 10,000 and 18,000 years ago is limited. Although there have been several research projects in the county over the past few years, only a small number of carbon dates exist for Lancashire and places of settlement are deduced from scatters of artefacts.

The area of Lancashire known as the Fylde lies between the River Ribble to the south and the River Wyre to the north, bounded on the west by the Irish Sea and on the east by the A6. The Fylde was a plain with islands of material laid down by glacial drift surrounded by hollow areas filled with peat. To the north of the river Wyre lay the extensive peat wetlands of Pilling, Rawcliffe and Winmarleigh mosses while to the south, in the area round Poulton, the proportion of wetland was less. People settled on the drier ridges with the wetlands providing peat for fuel and rough pasture for cattle in the summer months.

During the construction of new houses on a site on Blackpool Old Road Poulton in late 1997, a human skull was found in a trench dug in a layer of wood peat. This may have been a Bronze Age ritual burial of the skull of which there are other examples in the Fylde: the head of a woman was recovered from Pilling Moss in 1864 that had been buried in a woollen cloth with strings of jet beads and amber.

There is little evidence to provide information about settlements from these early times.

A pebble hammer found in Stalmine.

CHAPTER 2

From the Romans to the Normans

At the time of the Roman invasion in AD 43 the people of this area were part of a wider group living in the north of England known to outsiders as the Brigantes – a name suggesting 'upland people'. A smaller clan known as the Setantii have been identified as inhabiting the area lying to the west of the Pennines. Their name lives on in Portus Setantiorum – 'the harbour of the Setantii' for which Ptolemy of Alexandria provides the only written record. The exact site of this port is not known and the mouth of the River Wyre is only one of several possibilities. There is little doubt that Portus Setantiorum did exist, but the name implies that this would have been an important harbour and there is no evidence to suggest that the Fylde was a tribal centre for the Setantii which would have warranted the construction of such an important port. While it is more likely that the site of this harbour was further north, there is evidence that there may have been something near to the mouth of the River Wyre. Recent research suggests that the Roman presence in the Fylde area was greater than once thought. Roman coins have been found at Poulton, Skippool and Fleetwood; a hoard was discovered at Rossall in 1840 and another across the River Wyre near Hackensall Hall in 1926. The record of trackways also suggest there may have been a site near the coast. Coastal erosion is severe in this area and this may have long ago destroyed evidence of coastal sites.

There is little archeological evidence for the period following the end of Roman occupation in AD 410. Saxons had been brought into the country by the Romans in the early fourth century to cope with the growing threat from the Picts in the north. Place names give some indication of the Anglo-Saxon presence in Lancashire. One of the most characteristic place name elements is *tun* – denoting a farmstead or settlement: Poulton is the settlement by the pool, Marton – settlement by the mere, Thornton – settlement by thorn trees.

The parish church of Poulton is dedicated to St Chad, an unusual dedication for a church so far north. Chad was installed as the first bishop of Mercia with his see in Lichfield, but he was there for less than three years, dying of the plague in AD 672. Why was a church in Poulton dedicated to St Chad? There are just over eighty churches with this dedication in England. Of these about thirty-five have a pre-Reformation foundation and the majority of these old churches are close to Lichfield. We must assume that stories of Chad's life and miracles following his

*St Chad's church from
the Market Place.*

death had spread to the Fylde. It is likely that there was a church in Poulton before the Norman Conquest in 1066. Although the first existing written evidence of a church in Poulton dates from 1094 and suggests that it was built by Roger de Poitou, it seems unlikely that a Norman knight would dedicate a church to an Anglo-Saxon bishop.

In 1074 the land between the Ribble and the Mersey was detached from the diocese of York and transferred to the archdeaconry of Chester in the diocese of Lichfield, thereby becoming part of the southern province of Canterbury. Poulton, however, situated north of the River Ribble, remained in the archdeaconry of Richmond within the diocese of York. Distance made the archdeaconries of Chester and Richmond difficult to administer from their respective dioceses. Distinctions between north and south of the county continued until 1541 when the diocese of Chester was formed at the Reformation and all Lancashire joined in the one diocese, although retaining the same archdeaconries.

When the Domesday Survey was commissioned in 1086 the county of Lancashire did not exist, the land south of the Ribble – *inter Ripam et Mersham* (between the Ribble and the Mersey) was included at the end of the Cheshire records and the land north of the river appears as part of 'the king's lands in Yorkshire'. Sixty-five communities are listed as being in Amounderness but no details are given and all but ' Aschebi', which was somewhere in the Myerscough area, are still in existence. The survey records that all the villages and three churches belonged to Preston but it is probable there were more than three churches in existence in the hundred of Amounderness. Not all churches were entered in the Domesday records and Poulton church more than likely predates the Conquest. Only sixteen communities in Amounderness were inhabited at the time, the rest were 'waste', either laid waste as a result of William's efforts to gain control over the Midlands and the North in 1069-70, or were simply abandoned.

By the early 1090s Roger de Poitou was lord over a wide area of the north-west. The first mention of a church in Poulton is in a document of 1094 when Roger de Poitou granted St Chad's to the new priory of St Mary at Lancaster. 'He gave Poltun in Agmundernesia and whatsoever belonged to it and the church with one carucate of land and all other things belonging to it; moreover he gave the tithe of venison and of pannage in all the woods and the tithe of his fishery'. These rights were to be the focus of several disagreements over the centuries. There was difficulty in managing land many miles distant from the priory at Lancaster. On their frequent journeys to and from Poulton, Thornton, Singleton and Staining, the tenants and monks of the priory had to cross lands owned by the Banastre family who deeply resented the trespass. In 1276 Sir Adam Banastre and his followers attacked the Prior and his attendants on their way to Poulton and imprisoned them in Thornton. The king instigated an investigation, but no record of its findings survives. In 1330 arguments over trespass and the collection of tithes were finally settled. A road was made across the Banastres' lands running from Poulton and Thornton to Skippool and then across the River Wyre at the ford of Aldwath and on to Singleton. In return once the road was in place the Prior promised to withdraw all actions.

After the Conquest came a great monastic revival and the parish of Poulton became involved with two of the great monasteries in the north

The chapter house is all that remains of Cockersand Abbey.

There are many ruined buildings at Whalley that are worth a visit.

west. All that remains of the Premonstratensian Abbey at Cockersand is a small chapter house standing near the salt marshes just past the village of Cockerham. In contrast at the site of the Cistercian Abbey at Whalley, founded by the de Lacy family, the ruins of several buildings are still standing. Many acres of land in the parish of Poulton were donated to Cockersand during the thirteenth and fourteenth centuries by wealthy landowning families for the care of their souls after death and the Abbey at Cockersand thrived as a result of these gifts. The land was then rented out by the monks to be farmed by local families. The economy was predominantly agricultural and in order to succeed financially the monastic houses had to assist the inhabitants to exploit the land. Co-operation played an important role in the successful management of farming and freedom from paying tolls, fines and taxes allowed the monks to transport goods easily and cheaply. Through arrangements like these the abbeys and monasteries were funded and land was farmed successfully.

Gifts of land to the monasteries meant that granges had to be built to manage land often some distance from the monastery. Singleton was a grange of Cockersand Abbey and the abbot is recorded as paying 20s yearly for two ploughlands in the community which by 1297 had become known as Singleton Grange. Staining was the site of a grange of Whalley Abbey and was the hub of the abbey's agricultural organisation in the Fylde. The monks of Whalley had an agreement that they should have a half share of the marsh lying between Staining and Layton. They could draw water for their mill but were not allowed to take any fish. In 1348 the monks attempted to develop a weekly market at Hardhorn which would have proved useful for buying and selling the produce of their land at Staining, but it does not appear to have succeeded. Fisheries, windmills, marshes and water from Marton Mere are detailed in several documents relating to land and agreements in the area. Fisheries are listed in Singleton, Thornton and Marton and common pasture in Marton, Staining and Weeton. There was a horse mill at Staining and mills at Carleton and Thornton where there were also two saltcotes. Fishing was important with rights to 'free fishing', common pasture and the drawing of water together with the right to cut turf in Little Marton and from 'the Great Moss' which was at one time much larger than now.

Rent did not necessarily take the form of money. For the rent of a pair of white gloves, Henry, son of William, had a grant of water in the marsh

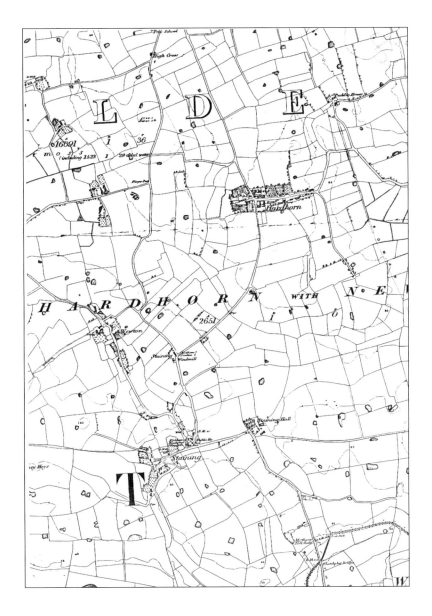

Hardhorn remains a small cluster of houses and farms on the 1848 OS map.

Thornton windmill retains its internal machinery and is open to the public.

between Little Carleton and Poulton an area which can be identified eight centuries later on the 1839 tithe map of Carleton. Over a dozen fields with the word 'marsh' in the name lie next to one another between Carleton and Poulton in the area of Fleetwood Road, together with Marsh Farm, near Amounderness Way. Fourteen acres of land in Little Carleton given to Cockersand Abbey by Isoud, daughter of Henry de Whittingham were described as ' abutting towards Bispham church' and may well be the three 'detached' areas of the township of Little Carleton which remained part of Bispham up to the early twentieth century.

CHAPTER 3

From Reformation to Civil War

In the sixteenth century Lancashire was among the poorest of the English counties and at times it was difficult for the community to maintain the fabric of the parish church. At such times money was raised by selling church property, a process which was continued at St Chad's into the nineteenth century. Thefts from churches were very common, with chalices, crosses and even bells disappearing. A ring of thieves operating in the Fylde was uncovered in 1535 who raided both Singleton and Lytham churches and others further afield; stolen chalices were taken to Penrith and sold to gold and silversmiths.

Regardless of personal beliefs everyone was expected to attend the parish church where all baptisms and marriages and burials had to be performed. Information about illegal churchgoers was collected. On 5 September 1538 an edict was introduced by Thomas Cromwell, Henry VIII's Vicar General: 'You and every parson vicar and curate shall for every church keep one book or register wherein ye shall write the day and year of every wedding christening and burying made within your parish for your time and so every man succeeding you likewise.' The incumbent and the churchwardens were responsible for the valuable church metalwork and fabrics and now the registers were to be kept with these treasures in locked church chests or coffers.

On the death of Henry VIII the Reformation gathered pace under the ten-year-old King Edward VI. Altars were taken down all over the country

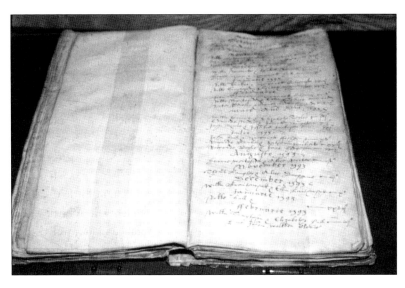

The earliest registers of St Chad's date from 1591.

This chalice may have been in use at St Chad's before the Reformation.

and in November 1550 they were officially abolished. In March 1551 it was ordered that all remaining church plate should be collected in to raise money for the king and the following year commissioners were appointed to compile new inventories and take charge of all plate and vestments leaving only the bare essentials for worship – a surplice, a couple of table cloths, a cup for communion and a bell. The survey carried out in 1552 recorded that at St Chad's there were: 'too chalyces iii lytle belles in the steple, copes iii albes a masse hud and stoyle whereof one is made of Red satyn, one of blewe buscyon, one of black chamlet and one checked vestment, one old cope.' The appointment of the Revd Ranulphe Woodward to St Chad's in 1552 was the last royal presentment by King Edward VI. A year later the young king's six-year reign ended with his death at sixteen and Mary ascended the throne. Churchwardens had then to set about replacing everything which had been removed, in some parishes a very expensive exercise, in others items from the church had been saved and hidden and could be used again. Others had sold them to use the money for the benefit of the parish. The traditional cycle of feast and fast days was ended leaving only the great festivals of Christmas, Easter and Whitsun and a few biblical saints' days.

In Lancashire Catholic priests were well organised and by the late sixteenth century there were over ninety households where seminarians could find shelter and help, thirteen of them in the parish of Poulton. Poulton was regarded as one of the most Catholic parishes in the county. In Lancashire Justices of the Peace appeared to be doing little to enforce the laws against recusancy and the ineffective administration and widespread Catholic sympathy meant that sanctions were applied haphazardly in the county. Common experiences forged bonds between the Catholic families in Lancashire and they were in close contact with one another, acting as guides for visiting priests, circulating news of drives against Catholics and ensuring the safe passage of letters.

In 1583 three or four masses were said each day in the Allen household at Rossall. William Allen was related to many of the Catholic families in the Fylde and there was some concern locally about Allen and whether he would become involved in planning a Spanish invasion on the Lancashire coast: 'touchinge a place called the Pille in Lancashire, a dangerous place for landinge. What the Spanyerd meanes to do the Lord knowes for all the countrye being knowen to doctor Allen (who was born hard by the pile) and the inhabytentes ther aboutes all ynfected wth his Romish poyson, yt is not unlyke yt his directione will be used for some landing there....' Born at Rossall in 1532, William Allen was made a Cardinal and died in Rome in 1594 where he is buried in the English church. In his will he left all his possessions to his parish church – St Chad's in Poulton – when England should again become a Catholic country but his possessions seem to have

St John's Catholic church was built in 1812 away from the road and hidden from view.

been dispersed at the time of the French Revolution.

At the Reformation St Chad's had become the Anglican parish church and Singleton became the centre for Catholic worship. The chapel there continued to be the focus for Catholics until the Jacobite rebellion of 1745 when it was wrecked and its contents stolen or destroyed. In 1812 it was decided to build a new church on land in Poulton lying between Moorland Road and the Breck given to the congregation by Thomas Fitzherbert Brockholes. The church, dedicated to St John the Evangelist, was opened in 1813. It was replaced in 1912 by a larger building designed by Pugin. In 1983 the old chapel became a listed building.

A tradition recorded in 1938 relates that in the previous century the Vicar of St Chad's had handed an old vestment to the Catholic church

The priest's house was incorporated into the building. This is now a listed building and is used as the church hall.

Alexander Rigby.

describing it as 'papist'. In a list of vestments at St John's church dating from the early 1830s there appears to be a reference to a vestment 'very old with grotesque figures' – maybe this confirms the tradition. Photographs of it were sent to the Victoria and Albert Museum in 1939 for identification and the vestment appears to be from the early sixteenth century with English embroidery (see colour section p. 3)

The 1640s saw several years of intermittent civil war and Poulton, like many communities in the Fylde, contributed its fair share of men to both parties and expressed no particular loyalty to either side. The Royalists included Alexander Rigby of Layton Hall, Captain Singleton of Staining Hall and Captain Bamber of the Moor – the area which formed the boundary between Carleton and Bispham. Enlisted for the Roundheads were Captain Richard Davis of Newton and Rowland Anyon of Thornton, both of whom raised companies in their own districts, under the command of Alexander Rigby of Goosnargh, cousin of Alexander of Layton Hall.

Though no engagements actually took place in or even near the town, one episode must have caused great local interest and some excitement. On 4 March 1643 a large Spanish vessel appeared close to the mouth of the River Wyre and rode at anchor there for several days, occasionally firing her guns. An investigating pilot boat found the crew ill and very weak, the firing of guns had been an attempt to ask for assistance. The ship was laden with ammunition intended for the Parliamentary forces in Lancashire. It was brought into the mouth of the River Wyre by Royalists and the crew were landed on the Rossall side and presumably told to fend for themselves. This tale has been the foundation for many supposed family secrets in Over Wyre communities as generations have spoken of the Spanish blood coursing in the veins of their dark-haired, olive-skinned relatives.

CHAPTER 4

Puritans, Methodists
and Congregationalists

Bishop Chadderton of Chester followed a policy of encouraging Puritanism in Lancashire, with programmes of religious instruction which included preaching sessions and prophesying on market days. Peter White, destined to be vicar of St Chad's for over sixty years, was presented to the vicarage of Poulton by Edward Fleetwood and instituted by Bishop Chadderton of Chester on 11 January 1583. In 1590 Peter White and other like-minded ministers compiled a report to be sent to the Ecclesiastical Court at York dealing with abuse of faith and morals. In August 1627 he was appointed to a commission by the Diocese of Chester for 'restoring spiritual jurisdiction to the Crown'. The members of the Commission had great power and much of the unpopularity of the Church at the time was in part due to the work of this Commission.

Several reports were to be prepared over the coming years on the religious and social condition of Lancashire, all complaining bitterly about the great number of Catholic priests to be found in the county, the 'heathenish and popish pastimes', unlawful trades and markets being held on the Lord's Day. 'The great tumultes of people remaining in the churchyard, streets and alehouses in the time of divine service from whence stones are oftentimes thrown upon the leaders of the church and many a clamourous noise and shout given out to the disquieting of the congregation'. The reports complained about the people clinging to the 'popish' parts of the services, corruption of the churchwardens and the parish clerks and the ruinous state of the churches, unrepaired and unfurnished. Fornication, adultery and drunkenness were said to be maintained by the multitude of alehouses, with 'seditious and mutinous talking by the alebench'.

Peter White and his wife had seven daughters and two sons. Four children, including the two boys, died in childhood, and three went on to marry local men, including Sarah who married Robert Freckleton, the minister at Bispham in 1634. By 1650 Peter White was described as being 'formerly an able and powerful minister but now very aged and infirme'. At this time he had held the living of Poulton for sixty-eight years so he must have been over ninety years old. A plaque with the name Peter White and the date 1622 is attached to the wall in the choir vestry in St Chad's but there is no record of what it commemorates.

A stone naming Peter White the longest serving vicar at St Chad's, though what it was commemorating is unknown.

In the aftermath of the Civil War, Oliver Cromwell, the great-great-grandnephew of Thomas, decreed that from 1653 all register keeping was to be taken away from the clergy and put in the hands of a layman who was known as the 'parish register'. Banns were still called in St Chad's, although Hugh Singleton and Margaret Lawson of Carleton had their banns called in the Market Place on 4 May 1656, market day. All marriages had to be conducted before the Justices and in Preston marriages were conducted before the mayor. St Chad's registers record at least ten marriages conducted at Barton Hall by Edward Hull on 13 May 1656 and marriages of other Poulton people were conducted at Preston by Mr Sherbourne JP. The clergy were replaced often by men with little training – 'tinkers, cobblers, saddlers, coachmen took on them the ministry of the word'. Homilies were provided to be read rather than allowing the clergy to preach sermons. In 1658 Cromwell died and with the Restoration of Charles II in 1660 the clergy went back to their parishes and the officials known as 'parish registers' were dismissed. Some of their record books were destroyed by the returning clergy. In December 1661 it was recorded in St Chad's parish registers that 'George Shaw had the Vicarage delivered to him'.

From 1672 licences were granted for dissident worship with individuals licensed for named premises. That year Cuthbert Harrison was licensed to preach at Singleton and Elswick chapel was licensed as a Congregational chapel. Over many decades licences were granted to several who did not wish to conform to the Church of England and wanted to set up other places of worship in the parish of Poulton. At the Quarter Sessions held in Preston on 10 October 1689 the barn and house belonging to John Sanderson of Hardhorn was to be appointed a meeting place for religious worship for those dissenting from the Church of England. In 1778 a revival began amongst dissenters with the coming of John Wesley, and other licences were granted, in January 1794 to use Robert Harrison's house and in 1799 John Gaskell's property.

In July 1807 a request was granted to use the house of James Morrow of Poulton, a dissenting teacher, as a Protestant dissenters' meeting place. James Morrow had been appointed to travel throughout the Fylde, particularly Kirkham and Poulton where he lived. In some places he preached to crowds of a hundred, but in 1808 the Lancashire Congregational Union reported on 'the Filde' that 'in a moral view this may be declared to have been the most dark and miserable part of the county. Mr Morrow has not been able to get a place to preach in Poulton and he therefore speaks in his own house which is but very small.' However a 'small commodious Independent chapel' was built at a cost of about £450 and opened on 11 April 1809. Over the years the chapel was to be closed for periods of time and was on one occasion used as a warehouse. In 1826 a letter said 'Poulton presents discouraging aspects. The friends at Marton and Bispham have left it, preferring Blackpool on account of its greater convenience.'

During the 1830s a religious revival began in Poulton with services being held in barns and cottages. An old farmer named Fairclough attached himself to the 'Particular Baptists' and began preaching, attracting quite a number of people and establishing a church. However after he died in 1886 the church ended and the group left Poulton. In 1886 the Independent chapel at Poulton was re-roofed and reseated for £195, making it 'one of the those comfortable little country chapels of which the denomination need not be ashamed.' But by the end of the century membership of the church had increased so that a new building was erected. Built of red brick and completed in 1899, it replaced the old chapel which was to be used as the Sunday school. The land for the new church was given by a local family whose house stood close by on Longfield Lane, the original name for the west end of Tithebarn Street. In October 1973 the Congregational Church merged with the Presbyterians to form the United Reformed Church.

The small Congregational chapel of 1818 and behind it the larger red-brick building which replaced it.

The Wesleyan Methodist chapel in Poulton – it was demolished in 1965, replaced by a new building on Queensway.

Methodists came from Preston to Poulton and Roger Crane is regarded as the founder of Methodism in the Fylde. He came to Poulton about 1784 but he was attacked by a mob when preaching in the Market Place, and rescued by a local boxer who recognised him. In the early 1800s a group of about a dozen met regularly in an outhouse at the back of the Kings Arms pub for prayer and Bible study, but they had to put up with persecution from the inhabitants. The group was regarded with suspicion and in 1811 the small room where they met was ransacked. Eventually a chapel was built in Back Street (later named Chapel Street) in 1819, only the second Methodist chapel to be built in the Fylde, after one erected at Thornton seven years earlier. Several joined the church during this period including John Sturzaker who later became a minister and Richard Seed whose slating business was on the Breck. In the 1830s Richard Seed together with his wife Catherine and sister-in-law Ellen Lewtas supported the Methodist church as it developed in Blackpool. Richard Seed often provided transport for visiting preachers between Blackpool and Poulton, taking candles and dusters with him to the chapel in Blackpool. Richard was later badly injured in a riding accident.

Although numbers were still small the Methodist chapel in Poulton was enlarged in 1861 and a Sunday school was opened with about forty-five children attending. An increase in the population of Poulton between 1880 and 1890 led the trustees to plan a new chapel to the north of the existing one with the original building accommodating the Sunday school. The reluctance of Mrs Grundy to sell her land alongside the church to allow the enlargements to take place was finally overcome by the diplomacy of William Tomlinson and three cottages and a plot of land were bought for £450 and the extension completed in 1909. William's son Robert Parkinson Tomlinson, a local corn merchant and a JP, was also a church member. Membership grew steadily and in 1964 a foundation stone was laid for the new church on Queensway, with the reference in its design to Poulton's maritime connections. The church was opened the following year and the original chapel was demolished and replaced by shops.

Quakers had visited Poulton and the villages nearby in the 1650s – Out Rawcliffe, Eccleston, Newton with Scales, Freckleton, Clifton and Wood Plumpton and a Fylde Monthly Meeting was set up, separate from Lancaster in 1698. In Poulton meetings were held in the houses of Henry Fleming, Daniel Weaver and Isaac Nickson, risking severe punishment if discovered; several members of the Moone family of Wood Plumpton were imprisoned in Lancaster. In October 1825 members of the Society of Friends applied for a house 'in a lane on the south side of the Market Place in Poulton' to be registered for worship and in June 1835 a Thornton Marsh Meeting was set up by John Warren, a visitor from America.

The difficulties of the Nonconformist preacher were varied. Moses Holden reported that 'At Bispham I was persecuted by the clergyman. One day when I had to preach there some of the people begged I would not go, for Mr Elston (vicar of Bispham) said he would have me put in prison. I said that would be an honour. I went and preached without any disturbance. Another Sunday Mr Morrow the Calvinist minister at Poulton sent word that I had better not go to Bispham, for he was well assured that the clergyman had engaged several men to kill me and they were to have ale and rum mixed to fit them for their work. Many came to persuade me not to go but I said 'I will go, I shall not be the first by many to suffer for the sake of Christ.' Two or three stout men refused to go with me for the clergyman had threatened to law everyone who had either lent me a chair or allowed me to stand on their horse block. So John Tomlinson took me in his shandry and I had it for a pulpit.'

CHAPTER 5

Brewing, Baking, Ditching and Threshing

The town plan of Poulton remained the same for centuries, a compact community surrounding the church. This aerial view was taken in 1932.

In medieval times the landscape of the country around Poulton and the River Wyre was open land with few trees or hedgerows, open fields and common meadows. Beyond this stretched moorland and marsh. The rough grassland provided valuable grazing for livestock in the summer months and the mossland provided peat and turf for fuel. This pattern can still be detected in Poulton. The Market Place itself was surrounded by houses, each with a small piece of land used for growing vegetables and fruit the keeping of geese, chickens, a cow or a few pigs. The last of these small allotments of land was finally lost when the Teanlowe car park was built in 1968. Beyond these gardens were open fields in all directions providing grazing for animals. Shippons dotted round the town, were used to house the stock in harsh winters and store extra fodder. Further out

Typically cottages were built with a wooden frame and a 'cruck' at either end.

from the town centre on the east side was the poorer quality grazing land, still marked by the position and name of Moorland Road. Beyond this was the mossland stretching out towards Singleton where peat and turf were dug for fuel and rushes gathered for floor covering.

More substantial housing was constructed using wooden-framed walls and crucks, infilled with wattle and daub, while the labourers' basic shelters were constructed of cobbles. Both had earth floors covered with rushes, thatched roofs and small, unglazed windows with shutters. The 'Fylde longhouse', a few of which have survived, consisted of the 'housepart', a large room with fireplace and chimney at one end used for cooking, eating and sleeping, and behind the fire a storage and food preparation room where bacon and dried beef would be hung. At the other end of the housepart were two small rooms side by side: one usually facing north was used as a buttery for dairy produce, the other was the parlour used to store valuable grain, tools and other valuables. This was probably where the owners would have slept. In later years a floor was often put in under the eaves to create attic rooms reached by ladders. The conditions in which labourers lived were harsh by modern standards, sleeping 'upon straw pallets, on rough mats onelie with a sheet under coverlets made of dagswam or hopparlots and a good round log under the heads in steed of a bolster or pillow, which was thought meet onelie for women in childbed. As for servants, if they had anie sheet above them it was well, for seldome had they anie under their bodies to keep them from the pricky straws that ran oft through the canvas of the pallet.'

In 1562 magistrates were empowered to fix the rate of wages and enforce them by fines or imprisonment. A penny an hour was deducted for absence and anyone striking was liable to a month's imprisonment and a fine of £5. If an employer gave higher wages than those fixed he was imprisoned for ten days and fined £5 and the worker served twenty-one days. The year was divided into two parts with a higher wage paid from 1 May to 1 October. It is estimated that it would have taken two days' work to buy one day's food illustrating the importance of payments from the poor rate and charities for labourer and his family.

An account of around 1600 gives a picture of a working day of a farmer or ploughman. He would rise at 4 a.m., feed the cattle, clean the stable and prepare the harness which took about two hours. Allowed half an hour for breakfast, he started work at seven with his horses or cattle until two or three in the afternoon. The team was brought home, cleaned and fed. After eating a meal himself he returned to the cattle at 4 p.m., gave them more fodder and prepared their food for the next day. After seeing to the animals again he had his supper at 6 p.m. then might spend the evening mending shoes for his family, beating hemp and flax, stamping apples for cider, grinding malt, picking candle rushes, or other husbandry tasks until 8 p.m. Finally he would take his lantern for a final visit to the stock and then to bed.

An order passed at the quarter sessions in Preston in April 1673 fixed wages to be paid to labourers in the adjacent hundred of Blackburn. The list gives a valuable insight into a wide range of skills needed by society in seventeenth-century Lancashire. A 'Bayliffe' was paid annually £3 10s, a miller £3, 'an ordinary servant in husbandry that can mowe and plowe well', £2 10s. A young man between the ages of twelve and eighteen years received 26s 8d, a woman servant 'that taketh charge of Brewinge, Baking and Kitchining, Milkehouse or Maltinge, 30s.' Others were paid per day: 'a mower of grasse, 12d, a man shearer or binder of corn, 4d, a man Haymaker, 3d, a woman, 2d, a Weeder of corn, 2d, Collier or workeman that is skillfull in getting of coaels, 10d'. The seasons brought variations in pay: 'Every man labourer for ditchinge, pailinge or raileinge hedgeing threshinge or other common labours from the Feast of All Saints to the first day of March shall not take for wages by the day with meate and drinke above 3d, And from the first day of March until All Saints with meate and drinke not above 4d.'

Practically the whole population of Poulton, which may have numbered around 500 people, depended on agriculture, with a few inhabitants having specific skills – smiths and millers, coopers, limers and thatchers. It has been estimated that in Lancashire fewer than one in a hundred could read and half that number were able to write. During the seventeenth century the inhabitants of Poulton suffered various

The surrounding hamlets consisted of farms for which Poulton supplied services and goods.

population crises as people did throughout Lancashire. A lack of any other supply of food in time of disease or famine and a shortage of medical care meant that many died young, famine leading inevitably to malnutrition and illness. In the years 1622 and 1623 there was an increase in the number of deaths recorded in the parish registers of St Chad's as in virtually every parish in Lancashire, with nearly three times the usual number of deaths. The cause was probably a mixture of malnutrition and disease; there is evidence that grain prices were on the increase at that time with famine further north. Wills record the need to provide for widows and children and this together with the relatively low value of property in the town suggests a population living at subsistence level.

A posed photograph illustrating the equipment once in common use for milking.

CHAPTER 6

Poverty, Crime and Punishment

Lancashire was governed by Justices of the Peace and a High Sheriff appointed by the Crown. JPs were landowners and leading merchants in the county who had property and money, social status and time to devote to the unpaid administration of the community. There were fewer JPs in Lancashire than any other county and for those who did take it on it became virtually a full-time job, meeting in session around the county in Manchester, Ormskirk, Preston, Wigan and Lancaster. They heard a wide variety of cases, settling disputes and dispensing justice. The system was helped by the appointment of local magistrates who met in their own homes to examine witnesses brought to them by the constable. Most crimes, thefts and brawls would be dealt with by local magistrates which involved them in taking evidence from the complainants and the constable. The assizes held in Lancaster Castle would deal with major crimes such as murder or large thefts.

Poverty in Poulton was addressed by distributing money collected from the poor rate. The Overseer of the Poor collected a compulsory poor rate and ensured its fair distribution, a difficult and unpopular post which no-one wanted. In 1697 Robert Taylor of Poulton had been appointed as Overseer of the Poor, a post he certainly did not want. He petitioned the Justices of the Peace, meeting at Preston, explaining that as a maltster his job was to service a kiln at Poulton which was a full-time job requiring his constant attention. The kiln's owner, Jonathon Blackburn Esq., lived thirty miles away and so relied on Taylor to do the job. His petition was successful – the JPs ruled that Richard Brown should serve in his place.

There were strict rules to determine eligibility for the parish poor rate, such as renting property in the parish for £10 or paying rates or working as a servant for a year. The provision of apprenticeships was seen as a useful method of dealing with young paupers who, as children and in the future as adults, could be a constant drain on the poor rate resources. Local tradesmen took on responsibility for their keep and taught the youngsters a trade. Strict agreements were put in place between apprentices and their master. In 1711 William Calvert was to be apprenticed as a cooper to James Rydeing of Poulton. William agreed that during the seven-year term 'the said apprentice, his master well and faithfully shall serve, his secrets and commandments (being honest and lawful) he shall willingly everywhere keep and do. The goods of his master he shall not inordinately waste or lend, fornication he shall not commit, at cards, dice or any other unlawful games he shall not play, from the service of his master he shall not depart nor absent himself without the licence of his said master but in all things as a good and lawful apprentice he shall justify and truly behave himself during the said term.' On his part James Rydeing agreed he would 'teach, instruct and inform his apprentice in the art or trade of a cooper, with a due manner of chastisement and shall give and provide unto his said apprentice good and sufficient meat, drink, washing and lodging, hats, shoes, stockings and all other apparel whatsoever both linen and woollen necessary and convenient for such an apprentice during all the said term of seven years.'

Often apprentices were sent to other towns to do their training, thus placing the future responsibility for providing poor relief on the other parish. An apprenticeship entitled an individual to a settlement certificate as did the parish where either the individual, or their father or husband, was born. People who became destitute in a parish for which they could not prove settlement would be issued with a 'removal certificate' and forcibly removed to the boundaries of the parish and sent on their way to their own parish of settlement, possibly hundreds of miles distant.

The case of Ann Andrews illustrates the law in action, taking on a caring role for the child but punishing the mother, in May 1692. 'Ellen Townsend of Medlar in Wesham widow who was midwife to Anne Andrews at the birth of her bastard child, Jennet the wife of Christopher Smith, who was midwife at the birth of the same bastard child, do upon their respective oaths said that the said Anne Andrews did in the time of her extremity say that John Whittle was the father of her bastard child. Anne Andrews being now asked who is the father of Elizabeth her bastard daughter, saith upon her oath that John Whittle, who was lately servant to John Whiteside of the Holmes within Thornton in the said county, yeoman, is the father of her said bastard daughter and that she hath no other father for the same. And farther saith that she believes that the said John Whittle now lives near Penwortham boat. The judgement was unanimous: 'Upon the evidence aforesaid we do adjudge John Whittle aforesaid to be the putative father of the said bastard child. And it appearing unto us that the said putative father is already absconded we do there upon hereby order that the said Anne Andrews be forthwith removed from Medlar in Wesham from where she now is, unto Poolton, being the place of her last legal sojourn and that the Overseers of the Poor in Medlar in Wesham do take care of the said bastard child until it attain to the age of fourteen years. And further that the Overseers of the Poor of Poolton, immediately after the receipt of the said Anne Andrews, do apply themselves to four of their Majesties' Justices of the Peace for a writ to convey her to the House of Correction, there to be punished according to the statute in that case made and provided.'

Justices also heard cases where the petitioner had been unsuccessful in getting help from the local Overseers. Janet Pearson's husband had fought for the Parliamentarians under Captain Richard Davie at both Lathom and Bolton in the Moors. On his return home to Poulton he had been taken away and imprisoned in Preston for his support against the King and Janet did not know if he was dead or alive. Janet's stepson James Pearson had forced her and her five young children out of the home in Poulton which was rightfully hers. Now destitute, she begged the JPs to summon James to account for his actions. During the sixteenth century local inhabitants had been given a variety of responsibilities for their community including poor relief, maintenance of the local roads, punishment of vagabonds and the destruction of vermin. To do this a constable, highway surveyors, assessors of meat and of bread, ale tasters and overseers of the poor had to be appointed. These were unpaid volunteers and many were reluctant to take on the roles. The township also meted out its own punishment; a ducking stool stood in Poulton at the bottom of the Breck where the offender was put in a chair suspended on a long pole pivoted over a pond and ducked into the water. As late as 1800 Jane Breckal had to parade round the inside of the church, clothed in white, bare footed and holding a candle in each hand as penance for misbehaviour, 'a spectacle of mirth to an unfeeling crowd'.

A constable was responsible for maintaining order in Poulton and investigations would take place the day following the misdemeanour.

The cross signified that a market was held in the town. This view is from around 1920.

Punishment when inflicted locally was immediate and could be very public. In 1626 William Lytham complained he had been cheated at cards by Arthur Smith in a Poulton inn the previous Christmas. Events such as this were viewed seriously at that time – the magistrates were concerned at unrest which might be encouraged by public meetings and regulation of alehouses was a main aspect of their work. Gambling was frowned on and was covered by bye-laws, as was football and other public entertainments. In 1627 William Wilkinson was brought before the JPs having accused Dorothye Shawe of being a witch and shouting after her in the street – a potentially dangerous situation to be in. Dorothy obviously felt it necessary to go straight to the magistrate before the rumours spread.

Elizabeth Johnson and Jane Clark, who with their husbands made a living by knitting stockings which they hawked round the country, were stopped by the constable in Poulton in June 1629 and set in the stocks as 'wandering persons'. On 15 January 1647 James Smith's shop in Poulton was the scene of a slanging match between Katherine and Isabel Swarbreck whose swearing and foul language saw them in front of Edward Rigby JP just three days later. On 11 November 1774 Jonathon Bell and John Smith, 'notorious vagabonds', were brought before Robert Gibson by the constable 'for divers notorious misdemeanours' and sentenced to be publically whipped at the Market Cross the following day.

In 1780 an Act was passed which established a Court of Requests for the speedy recovery of small debts in the parishes of Kirkham, Poulton Lytham and Bispham and the townships of Stalmine and Preesall. People were said to be running up small debts and then refusing to pay although they could afford to do so. The court was held once a week in Kirkham on Thursdays and in Poulton on Mondays. There was a strict code of conduct for the Commissioners – they were not allowed to 'keep any house of entertainment' or sell any wine or beer. Anyone summoned to appear before the court and refusing to do so was liable to be arrested and jailed for up to three months and have his goods sold to repay the debt.

CHAPTER 7

Life and Death

By the later years of the seventeenth century inventories of goods valued for probate show the wealthier inhabitants of Poulton enjoying a range of possessions and activities. John Dobson who lived on the Breck and died in 1664 had beehives and bees worth 10s and flax worth 8s, together with a variety of rods and sticks presumably to use with his stock. In his house he had pewter and wooden vessels, a chair, a stool and a trestle table, a bed with two sheets, a feather bolster and a bed cover, totalling for probate £8 7s 6d. In contrast James Taylor who died two years later was obviously a wealthier man, with a variety of livestock including oxen, cows, steers, heifers, nags and pigs. He had oats, hay and barley, cart wheels, wains, ploughs and harrows. His house was large, with a main room or fire house, two parlours, a brewhouse and a kitchen, three butteries, a milk house and a servant maid's chamber. Brass and pewter, five beds, five tables, chests and other furniture in these rooms and in other chambers were all valued for probate at £111 5s 2d.

Margaret More a 'widow of Pooltowne' died in 1669. Her house, which she rented from Alexander Rigby, stood 'at the Church Steele' an old name for an entrance to the church – this may have been the entrance from Chapel Street. Margaret More had a variety of possessions which could indicate she kept an inn: brass candlesticks, chaffing dishes and ladles, flagons, bowls, dishes, fire irons, spits, flesh forks, tongs and chamber pots;

There are four entrances into the churchyard. This one runs alongside a narrow passageway once known as Potts Lane, Potts Alley or Potts Entry.

beds, curtains, bolsters, blankets, covers, rugs and cushions. Flaxen sheets, pillows, towels, eleven other pairs of sheets, chests, boxes, tables, stools and feather beds were left to her three sons and her two-year-old granddaughter. Her best coat was left to 'Elinge and Jenet Walsh equally betwixt them'. The deceased's wearing apparel was often valued and included in the inventory and in 1789 Ellen Lewtas, a widowed bread baker, left her daughter Margaret Jump all her wearing apparel 'except some small part thereof which my younger son Thomas may choose to keep for his wife'. In fact it seems that Thomas never married.

Wills were only made by those with goods and possessions to leave. Generally these would be distributed by the will between relatives but for those with no family drawing up a will was an opportunity to show charity to the poor. James Baines was a woollen merchant whose house stood overlooking the Market Place. In his will of 1717 he left money to fund three Free Schools for poor children in the parish of Poulton, at Marton, at Thornton and at Poulton. All three are still in existence and after nearly 300 years, each is a successful modern school, still benefiting from the bequest of their founder. About 50 metres from Baines' window in the Market Place stood the ancient market cross and the fish slab, the whipping post and the stocks. At a time when there were the 'deserving poor' and 'undeserving poor' and begging was punishable by whipping, James Baines may well have watched punishment being meted out to child and adult alike in the Market Place and wondered at it. In his will dated 6 January 1717, just a week before he died, Baines left £800 to six trustees to be invested in land. Half the annual interest should be used for the poorest in Poulton who were not eligible to get money through the poor rate and

James Baines who died in 1717.

Baines' house overlooked the whipping post and stocks.

for putting poor children of Poulton into apprenticeships. The other half of the interest was to be spent on apprenticeships for the poor children of Marton, Thornton, Carleton and Hardhorn. James had bought land in Carleton in December 1711 at a cost of £315 and Carleton House Farm remained part of the estate into the late nineteenth century. Baines was a moneylender in the days before building societies and banks and he was owed over £2,350 when he died, secured by bills and bonds. Although there is no gravestone for James Baines to be found in St Chad's churchyard or in the church itself, that is not surprising. When the graveyard was closed and the inscriptions recorded in 1881 very few of the oldest stones were legible. The exact place of Baines' burial will remain unknown. However, it is entered in the burial register – 'Mr James Bayns of Poulton, buried January 12th 1717'. The trustees of Baines' charity were to dine annually on 21 December when the rents would be divided and other business transacted. The cost of the dinner in the 1820s was about 30s and this, together with 10s paid to one of the trustees for seeing to the accounts, was taken out of the rents each year. In the 1820s an average of seventeen apprentices were bound to trades, some found places in the township of Poulton but more were placed in the surrounding areas. In 1820 £14 was paid out for apprenticeships and the remaining money, amounting to £34, was paid out to poor inhabitants of Poulton. Similar arrangements were made in the other townships in the parish, Marton, Hardhorn with Newton, Carleton and Thornton.

Nicholas Nickson of Compley died three years after James Baines. After making provision for his wife during her lifetime, he decreed that after her death the income from the sixteen acres which he owned should be given to the churchwardens of St Chad's and the Overseers of the Poor in Poulton to be redistributed to poor inhabitants who did not qualify for relief from the poor rate. In carrying out Nickson's requirements a piece of land called Durham's Croft was purchased for investment. This land borders Higher Green and now forms part of the Park.

Edward Whiteside who died in 1721 also had land in Poulton, the rent from which he willed to be used to buy linen, woollen cloth and blankets for the poor. The trustees were to have either a coat or half a guinea each and a dinner on the day the cloth was bought, with entertainment for the trustees and a glass of gin for each recipient of the clothing.

The tradition of caring for the poor through legacies continued well into the nineteenth century. Mrs Catherine Dauntsey Foxton was related to two Poulton families, the Hulls and the Bucks. A memorial to these families is on the south wall of St Chad's church. Because of her family connections with Poulton and Blackpool in her will of 1878 she left £6,000 for 'a dispensary in Blackpool to provide for the poor residing in the parish of Poulton-le-Fylde and in the borough of Blackpool with medicines

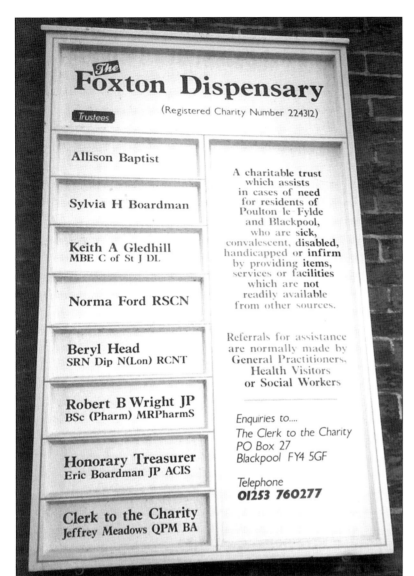

The public notice board in the Market Place gives details of this nineteenth-century charity.

and medical advice'. The Foxton Dispensary was originally set up in premises in Clifton Street, Blackpool, and later moved to Cedar Square, close to St John's parish church. The Dispensary now provides money for food, heating bills and other necessities. From medieval times the family home of the Bucks was Agecroft Hall in Pendleton, Manchester, a fourteenth-century half-timbered mansion. When William Hesketh Lever, later Lord Leverhulme, spotted it he ordered his architect to build a house in the same style at his new village, Port Sunlight. In 1926 the original Agecroft Hall was dismantled and shipped to Richmond, Virginia, USA, where it stands overlooking the St James River and is open to the public.

CHAPTER 8

A Georgian Church

By the early eighteenth century preaching had become an important part of church services and the nave of the parish church came to be regarded as the place for preaching with the pulpit an essential part of its furnishing. It was considered important that worshippers should be able to see and hear the officiating clergy so churches were comparatively small in size with galleries to accommodate as many as possible. Although Victorian antiquarians wrote that the church in Poulton was demolished and rebuilt in 1751, evidence which has come to light in recent years suggests that St Chad's was not completely demolished but drastically re-ordered inside to accommodate the new thinking. The outer walls, which are of red sandstone, were faced with grey ashlar at the same time.

There are only a few traces of the seventeenth-century church – some grave memorial plates and two plaques dated 1622 and 1638. The only description of the pre-1751 church at Poulton was written by the vicar of Whalley, Thomas Whitaker, in his *History of Richmondshire* published in

There is substantial evidence to suggest the church was not demolished and rebuilt from scratch in 1751, but extensively re-ordered over a period of four years.

St Chad's 'Georgian preaching box', in the 1990s. The centre aisle was put in during renovations in the 1950s.

1828: 'the old building consisted of a nave and north aisle and had four octagonal pillars extending from the chancel to the font with semi-circular arches between'. In 1990 as plaster was removed from the walls during repair work on the south-west wall of the gallery, a dark diagonal line running across the sandstone block was noted, thought to indicate the line of the medieval roof. The body of the church consists of red sandstone, which, according to Whitaker, was the fabric of the medieval building. Resurfacing the exterior of the church in large, grey ashlar blocks gave it the appearance of a Georgian church. But on 25 August

The galleries and box pews were built in 1751 and fit awkwardly across the windows. The ceiling was lowered in the mid-1840s.

1751 the vicar Robert Loxham inserted after the conventional entry of her baptism 'Margaret daughter of James Bisbrowne of Poolton', a comment; 'baptised at home by reason the church was down' which was taken by the Victorian antiquarians to indicate a complete razing to the ground. Evidence now suggests otherwise. During the year when the church was supposed to have been flattened a steady stream of thirty-six baptisms, eleven marriages and fifty-two burials were performed by the vicar with no further comment. James Bisbrowne, father of Margaret was apparently able to persuade the vicar to baptise his daughter in his own house even though other ceremonies were taking place in the church. James was an educated man, a house carpenter living on the Breck, and when he died in 1783 he owned ten cottages, a shop, gardens and shippon, as well as the tools of his trade. He was related to other well-established and influential families in mid-eighteenth-century Poulton. Perhaps he was actually conducting the building work which was going on at the church in 1751 and did not want his daughter to be baptised amid the dust and dirt?

The faculty issued in 1751 giving permission from the Diocese of Chester for the work to go ahead simply mentions various smaller projects. A gallery then on the east wall was to be removed and re-erected on the west wall; two additional galleries were to be built on the north and south walls; the pulpit would be repositioned; two staircases built; and financial arrangements made to pay for the work. It seems that part of the cost of the work was raised by a national public collection or brief, but the local farmers apparently having pocketed the proceeds, the money had to be found through private contributions and collections. Rather than a complete rebuild it would have been very much cheaper to adapt the

A diagonal line on the west wall may have been the medieval roof-line. It is now hidden inside a storage cupboard.

The west wall in the roof space shows how the tower walls of sandstone and brick were amalgamated.

existing structure, retaining the original walls, door and window spaces, and the evidence suggests this was done. The present windows, which reach from about five feet above the ground almost to the roof must surely have been in existence before the erection of the side galleries, which are simply attached rather precariously to the wall by beams, leaving a large gap between the galleries and the windows. The four main windows, two each in the north and south walls, are not in alignment with each other. If the church had been newly-built to a modern design in 1751, the windows and galleries would have been designed as an integral part of an overall plan, rather than with galleries clumsily crossing over the window space and blocking much light. It was not until the nineteenth century that three small oval windows, one on the north side and two on the south, were inserted high in the walls to admit more light to the galleries. Other evidence supports this interpretation. The visitation records show that the work at St Chad's was spread over a period of at least four years during the 1750s. In 1750 the churchwardens wrote that 'Our church is not in so good repair as we would wish it, but we are preparing with all expedition we can to make it in sufficient repair'. In 1752 they reported that 'Our church is rebuilt but not finished', and it was not until 1754 that they were able to record 'Our church is rebuilt and finished'. Robert Loxham died in 1770, still holding the position of Vicar of Poulton. He is buried, together with numerous other family members, in the churchyard at Kirkham, his birthplace.

With the pulpit now placed centrally, all worshippers had a good view of the preacher wherever they were seated, a design Sir Christopher Wren thought 'beautiful and convenient'. Later in the eighteenth century the pulpit was combined with a reading desk and a seat for the clerk from

The pulpit was made in 1955 from panels of an original Jacobean pulpit that had been hanging on the south wall since the 1880s.

The initials of six churchwardens on a stone. There is no record of the event which caused this to be carved.

The tower is thought to date from the mid-seventeenth century and was untouched in the alterations of 1751.

where he lead the responses and the singing, so the pulpit was transformed into the magnificent three decker structures of which some still remain. The tiny old church of St John in Pilling is a good example of a smaller Georgian church still with its gallery and a small three decker pulpit. St Chad's was filled with box pews, their high wooden walls and small doors designed to keep out cold drafts in the unheated church.

The tower of St Chad's parish church predates the work of 1751 but there is no evidence to set a date for its building. The south side of the nave is in line with the south wall of the tower and an arched doorway, now blocked up, is all that remains of the original entrance from the church to the bell tower. A plaque rediscovered in 1836 when the pulpit

The fields that surrounded Poulton can still be seen in this view from the tower taken in the 1930s.

was moved has six sets of initials and the date 1638. What the plaque commemorates is unknown; local tradition has it that it marks the building of the church tower, but there is no evidence for the claim. There are eight bells, six of which were cast in 1741 by Abel Rudhall of Gloucester. These are inscribed 'Prosperity to all our benefactors AR 1741', 'Peace and good neighbourhood AR 1741', 'Prosperity to this parish AR 1741', 'When you ring us we'll sweetly sing AR 1741', 'Abel Rudhall cast us all at Gloucester 1741'. This last bell was re-cast in 1865 and paid for by the Vicar, the Revd Thomas Clark. It carries the names of the vicar and churchwardens. The bells were re-hung in 1908. In 1937 two new bells were dedicated and hung in the church tower.

The view from the top of the tower is well worth seeing. A visitor in the 1870s recorded sights some of which are long gone: 'Fleetwood with its regular masonry and sharp mastheads, the bay of Morecambe with its belts of sand, the heavy smoke from the smouldering furnaces of Barrow, the rugged and romantic mountains of Westmorland and Cumberland, the labyrinthine hollow in which Preston seems to sit moodily with its factories, Longridge Fell, Pendle and Rivington Pike, North Meols and Southport make a faint light line on the eastern edge across the estuary of the Ribble. Lytham dreams on in its selectness and salubrity, Blackpool rises like a dark stately promontory of masonry to the south west. The intermediate space is filled in with villages and wide expanses of agricultural land ... and ... fourteen windmills.' The view no longer includes smoking furnaces of Barrow, wide expanses of agricultural land or fourteen windmills. The farms of Poulton and Carleton have almost all been covered by housing, built to accommodate those now wishing to live in Poulton, and the windmills are demolished or turned into monuments and unusual homes.

A recent view shows the development that has taken place in the town centre.

Box pews in the north gallery, with a seat at the back for family servants.

Hewitson, a journalist with the *Preston Pilot*, attended a service at St Chad's one Sunday in 1871. His report, written with tongue in cheek, describes the parishioners as he saw them that day: 'The young and ancient maidens, the sedate and demurely attired, the dignified folk who sat alone amid much piety and starch in select pews, goodly faced old farmers, kindly eyed old matrons who cropped up in plenteousness, patriarchal men who sleep much during service time and blame other folk for not keeping awake. The reading was clear and regular .... the preaching excellent .... the clerking was tolerably done.' He kept his wrath for the choir, 'The singing was weak, emaciated, unartistic .... entirely devoid of force as if the members of the choir were swooning and needed a sudden nipping or hitting or frightening to stir them into life.' Although the box pews on the ground floor and the west gallery were removed from St Chad's in 1885, the two side galleries still contain the original eighteenth-century box pews. Those on the north side have a 'back seat' for the servants, those on the south wall are a simple rectangular box. Hewitson observed, 'The box pews were of various makes and shapes – broad and narrow, open and closed, high and low. Near the pulpit were several high walled box pews looking very foolish and antiquated and constituting a complete eye sore. They ought to be taken out altogether'. The family pew of the Heskeths came in for some acerbic criticism: 'An elaborate arrangement reaching from the floor to the gallery, aristocratically isolated, looking like a cross between a railway carriage and the centre piece of a gondola and dignified enough to be the sitting place of the Tycoon of Japan.'

Apparently Hewitson's views about the dated appearance of the church interior were shared by the parishioners. In 1885 a major re-ordering was

St Chad's in around 1900. The first organ was installed in 1828 and the present one dates from 1912.

undertaken which brought about, amongst other changes, the movement of the pulpit and the replacement of the ground floor and west gallery pews. The Hesketh family pew was moved to the southwest corner where two sides were used as screens to form the baptistry. The Vestry consented to the Vicar choosing for himself sufficient from the old pews to panel a parish room at the vicarage. Unfortunately this panelling was lost when the vicarage was demolished in 1955. In this re-ordering one of the two sides of the Hesketh pew was replaced with new wooden panelling so that today only a small part of the screen remains. The family pew of the Rigby family also stood against the south wall until 1885.

Music and chant were important in parish worship as early as the fifteenth century. Wealthier members of the parish gave large sums of money towards intercessions and others established institutions which supported and trained the clergy and choristers. Chantries were established in parish churches where the presence of a priest, often competent in music, was stipulated to celebrate a daily Mass for the founder and the departed. There was a chantry in Poulton church in the fifteenth century probably founded by the Thorneton family, in 1414 John de Thorneton was buried there. The small organs which had been in use in medieval times were destroyed when the Puritans tried to forbid the use of them altogether. In 1644 an order stated that 'all organs and the frames or cases wherein they stand in all churches and chapels shall be taken away and utterly defaced and none hereafter set up in their place'. By the seventeenth century choral singing had developed as part of church worship and musical instruments provided a natural addition to the singers in St Chad's as in other parish churches. There seems to have been an organ in St Chad's from around 1780 which then brought added

Robert Hornby Porter.

expenses. Possibly the entry 'Sundry expenses about the organ £10 5s 7d' refers to its purchase and setting up in the church. There are other charges associated with it: 'Organist £5 2s 6d and organist's salary £15 15s 0d'. A note appeared in the churchwarden's accounts: 'It is agreed this day amongst the parishioners of the several townships of the parish of Poulton that all charges of the organ and the organist for the parish church of Poulton shall not be defrayed hereafter by a tax levied on the parish generally but by voluntary subscriptions only'. Soon afterwards a singing master was hired at an annual cost of £15 15s.

The simple band with a group of singers in the west gallery, known as the singing pew, became a common feature of churches towards the end of the eighteenth century. Most of the composers were amateurs and the music produced included local and traditional hymns and music popular with ordinary people in the parishes. In 1840 a violoncello was bought for St Chad's at a cost of £5 2s 6d, paid for by the sale of the old organ to Thomas Hardman, landlord of the Green Man, for £3, the rest being made up with subscriptions. Maybe the musicians and singers provided the music for the next few years – it was not until 1855 that a new organ was bought, the money for it having been having been raised by public subscription. The clergy generally were concerned that church musicians were just as likely to play their instruments for local dances as for church services and in many churches changes were put in place to remove the musicians from the galleries and bring the singers and organs down to the ground floor where they could be watched. By the early years of the nineteenth century the singers in St Chad's were located downstairs in a singers' pew. Then, as part of the major re-ordering which took place in St Chad's in 1885, in what was considered to be a more seemly

An early picture of St Chad's before the apse was built in 1868.

arrangement, the organ was moved from the west gallery to the ground floor and placed in a new area at the north east end of the church created by removing the staircase at the end of the north gallery. The singers were replaced by a robed choir in new choir stalls standing opposite the organ. Some years later in 1891, it was decided 'in order to improve the musical portion of the service' to disband the old mixed choir and form a new one of men and boys dressed in surplices. In 1912 the old organ was replaced with a larger instrument at a cost of £500 plus the old organ in part exchange. It was hand-blown until 1929 when an electric blowing plant was installed.

A visitor to a service in St Chad's in 1871 sat at the back on the north side and later remarked that the area which was 'pestilently noisy, contained a variety of lads who talked and laughed and hit one another on the head'. He afterwards found out it was called 'Brutes' Corner'. In fact discussion had already taken place on the unsuitable position of the churchwardens' pew; several of the wardens complaining that they were unable to hear anything because of their proximity to the children who were in the habit of making a considerable noise during the services. Robert Hornby Porter was a musician and played the bass violin for services in the west gallery of St Chad's. It was said that his presence in the music pew at St Chad's ensured good behaviour from the children in church. He served Poulton well in a variety of roles. He was the registrar of births and deaths, and a newspaper correspondent passing news of Poulton people and events to the newspapers based in the large town and cities – such as the *Preston Pilot* and the *Liverpool Mercury*. He was also Superintendent of the Sunday school and Overseer of the Poor and officiated at the fortnightly meetings which doled out poor rate to the needy.

The altar in St Chad's originally stood against the east wall, but in 1868 an apse was added to the east wall, paid for by the vicar the Revd Thomas Clarke. Some graves had to be removed from in front of the east wall where the apse was to be built and £3 was kept by the churchwardens to be given to the representative of the Addison family if demanded, in leiu of iron rails and stone pillars which had been removed from the site of the new chancel. There is no record of the offer having been taken up.

An article in the *Preston Pilot* of 22 August 1840 reported: 'Last week some workmen digging a foundation on the property of Mr Banks at Poulton met with what they supposed to be a large stone mortar. It however proves to be an octagonal font of comparatively small dimensions having engraved upon it a cross the letters MH and the date 1649. It evidently has been fastened with lead on a pedestal. The place where this antiquity was discovered being a hollow was filled up with the rubbish of the old church, which fact will satisfactorily answer for its

Lucy Hall, daughter of the vicar, painted this view for the family cook in 1858.

The plaque from Alexander Rigby's town house together with what was once thought to be an old font.

being found on ground occupied by buildings. It is in the possession of the Revd W. Thornber of Blackpool'. The history of fonts in St Chad's is confused, but it seems likely that this one had been in the church in 1649 and was removed in 1751 at the time of the major reordering of the interior to be buried along with other 'rubbish'. Later records show that in 1885 this font was presented by Giles Thornber, William's son, to the vicar of the time, the Revd William Richardson. In 1871 the second font was removed from the church and sited on the west lawn of the vicarage, to be replaced in St Chad's by one in memory of Frances Mary who had died in 1866, a daughter of the Revd John Hull. As the Hull family had left Poulton two years previously the family must have felt a particular affinity with St Chad's to make the presentation of a font in memory of their daughter. In 1858 another daughter, Lucy Hull, painted a picture of St Chad's as a present for the family cook. In 1964 the cook's granddaughter presented the painting to the church.

In 1874 a cover was made for the old font which stood in the vicarage garden it and a bottle and documents were placed in it as a memento of the occasion. Strangely the record of this ceremony does not appear in the churchwardens' accounts until eleven years later in 1885. In the mid-1880s a good deal of work was carried out inside the church and perhaps questions were asked about the ownership of the old font leading to the event being at last recorded. The font dedicated to Miss Hull remained in the baptistry until 1932 but its whereabouts now are unknown. It was replaced in 1932 with a fourth font provided by the Haworth family who were originally of Whitworth and this one is still in use today.

CHAPTER 9

The Market Place

In the mid-eighteenth century the Market Place was surrounded by a number of low thatched cottages with the Moot Hall standing with its back to the churchyard. In the nineteenth century a large three-storey building stood here. Shambles and penthouses stretched out in front of the property on both sides of the Market Place. There were no raised pavements but stepping stones enabling walkers to manoeuvre their way between the mud, manure and drain water which mingled freely in the streets. A few private residences stood out from the rest because of their large size and their slate roofs. The town house of the Rigby family stood on Bull Street, facing the church across the Market Place. A plaque with the arms and the date 1693 was once fixed to the front of the property, now to be found at the foot of the church tower on the south side. The house passed out of the hands of the Rigbys shortly after Sir Alexander's death in 1717. In the early years of the nineteenth century the house was

One of the earliest photographs of Poulton, taken before the lamp commemorating Queen Victoria's Golden Jubilee (1887) was in place.

Alexander Rigby's town house with the family coat of arms. The building later became a bank.

used for a business involved with flax dressing and twine spinning.

The house became a branch of the Lancaster Bank in 1898 and in 1907 was rebuilt. The original house was typical of the period in which it was built with massive thick walls, many of which were made of stout staves, plastered over with clay. Laths and plaster were added in later years. It had an outside staircase of stone, leading to the upper rooms, which were probably originally used as storerooms. The inside staircase was of fine solid oak. During the process of demolition a very small room lit by a tiny window, thought to be a priest hole, was found near a fireplace.

A detailed list of property in Poulton forming part of Sir Alexander Rigby's estate dates from around 1714 and lists in Poulton twenty-nine houses with gardens, sixty-four acres of land, a horse mill – possibly standing in a field at the bottom of the Breck – and a shop and stable. Most landowners had no other means of investing so their income came from letting land. Regular collection of rents and good accounting was essential to the smooth running of the estate.

A recurrent theme running through many of the town's records is money. The difficulties of collecting it from unwilling inhabitants and of spending it wisely, addressing the needs of the town and the church, the great public building in the town centre. By the eighteenth century there was a public recognition that, like individuals, communities could be hit by events so catastrophic that they were unable to deal with the problem without help. Common practice was to send out a national appeal for such serious devastation. Known as 'briefs', these were appeals for money to be given by the public, announced by the clergy in church and collected across the country at a central point from where the money would be sent to the affected place. In 1732 Poulton itself was suddenly in need. In the tradition of the time mourners would follow a funeral with lighted tapers as the procession moved through the Market Place to the church. It proved disastrous on 3 March 1732 at the funeral procession of Geoffrey Hornby when sparks from the tapers set fire to the thatched roofs on the west side of the Market Place. The whole row was destroyed and the inhabitants could only stand and watch as the place went up in flames. The collection to help in financing the rebuilding did not go out until 1736 and it was estimated that it would cost £1,060 to rebuild the whole of the west side of the Market Place. The resulting block of property still retains its uniform appearance.

A hand-loom weaver.

Over the years people of Poulton responded to appeals for financial assistance from all over the country and even further. They contributed to Colchester, Wetherby chapel and Wallazea (Wallasey), they sent 12s 10½d to Lytham church in 1766 and £1 0s 9d to Padiham in 1763. Appeals came in from further afield – Philadelphia, New York and Westphalia. As late as 1862, with concern spreading for those employed in the cotton industry in Lancashire, suffering in the wake of the American Civil War and the resulting shortage of cotton imports, a house to house collection was made in Poulton with collecting boxes in each church, the money paid into a Central Relief Fund in Manchester.

Many churches still have their Briefs Book listing the collections made over several years in the eighteenth century. In 1990 an appeal was received at St Chad's from the churchwardens of St Laurence, in Steppingley, Bedfordshire, who were raising money for the repair of their church roof. A look through St Laurence's eighteenth-century Briefs Book showed that in 1736 they had collected 6d to help Poulton with the rebuilding – and now they were inviting St Chad's to do likewise. St

When this shop roof was being repaired in 1990 some of the timbers were found to have been re-used after the fire of 1732.

Chad's duly responded and St Laurence's successfully paid for the repair to their church roof, with the help of these reciprocal gifts. Later in 1990 the butcher's shop in the Market Place was being re-roofed. With the slates removed it was easy to see the new light wood beams next to the large old dark wood they were replacing. Once the original wooden beams were brought down they revealed large nails, wooden pegs, joiners' marks and, most fascinating of all, signs of burning at one end. Some of the wood had obviously been reused for the new building after the fire of 1732.

Each parish had a 'governing body', a group of men who acted on behalf of the parish. The earliest record of this group in Poulton is in a document dated 9 December 1623. 'It is generallie considered, agreed and set down, by Thomas Singleton, of Staining, Esq., and the rest of the parishioners and other inhabitants, together with the churchwardens and Four-and-Twentie Men of the Parish of Pulton and Peter White, the Vicar of Pulton that . . . Thomas Dickson, the younger . . . Be clerk of the Parish of Pulton.' After this the records are silent on the subject of the Twenty Four Men until the year 1708, after which, on each of three consecutive years, the churchwardens' minute book records a general meeting at Easter of the 'Vicar, Churchwardens and Twenty Four Men of this p'sh of Poulton' to determine the amount to be 'assessed and collected within our said p'sh for the repairs of the Church and other necessarys relating thereto.'

The parish church in many communities was the largest and most important building. The churchwardens' main role was the maintenance of the fabric and furnishings of the church and two churchwardens were appointed annually from each of the five townships at St Chad's Easter vestry meeting and the names of those elected recorded in the minutes.

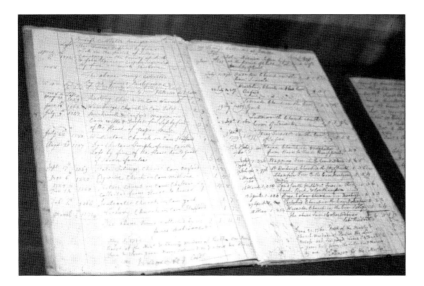

The churchwardens' accounts do not begin in detail until 1760.

The election of the churchwardens of St Chad's still takes place in April each year before the annual general meeting of the Parochial Church Council. The churchwardens were entrusted with money collected from the townships for the upkeep of the church and therefore their accounts had to be kept carefully. The first surviving documents kept by the churchwardens of St Chad's date from 1710 and are simply a record of those elected to the office. The few pages which remain from these early eighteenth-century documents were, in the nineteenth century, bound in with the later volumes which begin in 1764. The issues which appear in the churchwarden's account year after year, build a picture of life in Poulton over a period of almost 300 years.

In the early eighteenth century the only income for the upkeep of St Chad's was an annual payment made by each of the five townships. In 1708 it was agreed that for the five townships of 'Poulton, Stayneing, Marton, Carlton, Thornton: 24 men of this parish ordered and agreed the sum of £33 15s shall be assessed and collected within the said parish for the repair of the church and the necessaries relating to the year.' In 1710 the sum was increased to £35 10s, a figure which continued unaltered for many years. Many local people were employed to carry out repair and maintenance work on and around the church and they presented their bills regularly to the churchwardens: 'Thomas Stables for bell Roaps 10s 6d, Thomas Wilde for paving 6d, Thomas Santer for work in church yard 6s, Hugh Seed for flagging £6 18s 8d, Richard Jackson for carting flags £1 7s, Thomas Crook for church steps 18s 4d, James Crookall for a gate stoop for church gate 2s.' Thomas Santer earned 1s for mowing the churchyard. The needs of all these workers were catered for and in place of the present day cups of tea, they had ale – 'allowance for ale for workmen 1s 10d'. The

A clock made by Samuel Lomas, a renowned clockmaker who lived in Sheaf Street.

church clock gave regular work to Samuel Lomas, a clockmaker of some renown in the county, who lived in Sheaf Street. 'To Mr Lomas for mending Clock etc. 2s 2d ... Putting up clock 3s ... Putting up ladder 6d ... Mr Lomas for clock finger and repair of the clock this year and last.'

The poor condition of the roads meant the rushes placed on the church floor to mop up the mud and rainwater needed to be changed regularly and the floor swept with besoms. It cost money to replace the rushes – 'cartage of rush 6s 6d, Sam taking rush out of church 1s 6d', a process which went on until the early years of the nineteenth century. Throughout the year, but particularly for important festivals, much cleaning went on for which people were paid: 'Cleaning candlesticks 2s, Scouring pewter 2s 6d, Cleaning windows 7s, Cleaning the bell loft, Cleaning and washing church after the white limers 1 6d, Clerk's wife cleaning church and church plate 3s 3d, Washing surplices 4s, Cleaning pewter 5s, Lomas cleaning clock 1s, John Santer for cleaning shandilears 3s'. Perhaps this was too big a job for one man, for two weeks later, '16 December cleaning shandileers 3s'.

In the eighteenth century the service of the Eucharist took place only a few times during the year and costs of between 10s and 13s were recorded on each occasion. Wine for communion cost 6d and Thomas Lewtas a breadbaker with his bakery in Sheaf Street in the late eighteenth century provided bread for the communion at a cost of 3s. Provision for services and festivals included regular purchases of candles bought in bulk – 5cwt cost 2s 11d. A new prayer book and carriage to bring it to Poulton cost £1 1s 3d; a new communion cloth £1 10s 3d; a marriage register book 16s 3d. Books for services including a new version of the psalms at 2s, a prayer book and 'four books of the general form of prayers as approved by government.' Furnishings and fittings were made and cared for by the parishioners. Mr Warbrick charged 11s 4d for a new table cloth and 10d for cloth for a surplice; George Walmsley made window curtains and rings for the east window at a charge of 2s 6d.

From 1538 the clergy were required to enter all christenings, weddings and burials in registers and from the late sixteenth century there had been an annual requirement that a good copy of all register entries for the previous year should be made at Easter and sent to the Bishop. These documents have survived as Bishops' Transcripts and are now a source of important material when original parish registers have been lost. Mr Woods was paid 8s each year for copying the register for which he needed one quire of paper for 10d and a bottle of Indian ink for 6d. The Clerk was paid £8 16s 6d for his year's work in 1767 – over 20 per cent of the total annual income for the church. Annual visitations or court cases could mean that the churchwardens had to go to Preston. In 1767 their expenses amounted to £1 7s 5d with 2s 6d to hire a horse for the curate, and court fees of £1 19s 6d. Occasionally the churchwardens had expenses for other items – 'a meeting, sending for boys that had done mischief at church 1s.' Later it was agreed that 'the Churchwardens' expenses on every visitation shall on no pretence exceed 40s'.

Although the churchwardens were elected annually as upstanding reliable and trustworthy men, there could be the occasional problem even with officers of the church. In 1805 John Santer, the clerk, was convicted of getting himself drunk and John Swarbrick of 'making hindrance' and they were each fined 5s in the court at Garstang. On other occasions Andrew Simpson and John Benson, William Whiteside and William Hodgkinson were all before the court at Garstang for drunkenness and Thomas Gardner was ordered to appear before Mr Bourne, the magistrate, for being drunk in the church.

Occasionally it is possible to date a particular addition to the church from these accounts – in 1787 William Brown was paid £1 5s 1d for building an external door into the tower. Before this the only way in had been an ancient doorway leading from the church. The old entrance was blocked up when the external door was made in 1787 but its outline is still visible in the tower.

CHAPTER 10

Bells and Burials

The life of an eighteenth-century preacher in the Fylde was recorded in the diaries of the Revd Peter Walkden a non-conformist minister of Thornley near Chipping. Twice during 1733 he travelled to preach at Bispham, and called at Poulton, on the second occasion taking his wife with him to see the sea for the first time. There they heard of the death of Robert Mercer, the vicar of Great Eccleston, who had gone the previous week to 'bathe and take the air about Poolton'.

St Chad's bells were rung on special occasions such as the birthday of the monarch, for which the ringers were paid 3s. The bellringers and the singers were paid a basic fee of about £1 16s a year for each group but they also earned extra together with free ale for special events and services such as that marking 5 November and the monarch's birthday. By 1784 the costs of paying the bellringers and the churchwardens' expenses had been a concern. 'It was agreed at the vestry meeting that in future the public ringing days in the parish shall be reduced to two – namely the King's birthday and Christmas, the ringers be allowed 5s each on each day. On 9 November 1805 the bells rang for Lord Nelson's victory at Trafalgar, but the following year it was decided that 'no money should be given to the ringers on the account of any victory in future on the parish account'.

Some of the entries in the churchwardens' accounts are cryptic: '2 February – on a very cold day we spent 6d' and the phonetic spelling

A small brick building on the far right housed the church's horse-drawn hearse during the early nineteenth century.

looks odd to modern eyes: 2lb ogslard, 2s 6d for cleaning the shandilears and 10s per annum rent for the 'herst' house. In the mid-eighteenth century payments of rent for the 'herst house' rent began to appear regularly in the accounts. The spelling at first proved a puzzle – what was the 'herst' or occasionally 'erse' house? When James Bisbrowne became clerk, his better command of spelling made it clear that it was a building in which a hearse was kept. Burials in St Chad's or in the graveyard brought in extra revenue; to be buried inside the church cost 6s 8d while burial in the churchyard cost 3s 4d. Once the parish had its own hearse charges could be made at 3d per mile to bring back to St Chad's deceased parishioners who lived some distance from Poulton or who had had the misfortune to die in another parish or even another town. The hearse went all over the locality – to Larbreck for Richard Harris 1s, to Pilling for William Hodgson's mother-in-law 2s, and to Elswick for Mrs Brown 1s 3d. But it also went much further afield than the local parishes – Thomas Lewtas paid 12s 6d for the hearse to go to Manchester, the hearse went to Blackburn for Margaret Row 7s 3d, and trips to Blackpool, Bispham, Kirkland, Marton, Englewhite, Garstang and Preston are all recorded. In the early months of 1815 the hearse also provided a service for members of the Catholic chapel at Singleton, travelling to and from Elswick, Clifton, Plumpton and Highmoor.

Although the new Catholic church at the bottom of the Breck had already been built on land given by Thomas Fitzherbert Brockholes and had been opened in 1813, the first burial did not take place there until May 1815. In spite of the costs involved – in 1785 Richard Abram was paid 7d for repairs to the 'herst' saddle and in 1806 horse gears cost £2 9s 10d plus the 10s annual rent for the hearse house – the hiring out of the hearse must have helped with the upkeep of the church. The hearse continued to travel even further – to Preston, Blackburn and Liverpool. There were several Poulton families who had moved to Liverpool to become involved in shipping and trade, but they still felt their roots were in Poulton and wished to be buried there. As early as 1781 the hearse had gone to Liverpool for Mrs Thornber. When a request for a public subscription was issued in 1854 for the purchase of a new organ, of the 173 people who subscribed to the total of £267 15s, 48 of them were recorded as 'of Liverpool'.

As the nineteenth century progressed professional undertakers set up in business making St Chad's hearse redundant. In 1847, nearly eighty years after it was first used, the churchwardens decided that 'if the hearse be not called for by a parishioner before the 20 September next it be disposed of for the benefit of the parish'. Three weeks later the whole lot had been sold for £2 16s, less 5s for the auctioneer's charges. The hearse house itself, which was in Burlington Terrace, survived until the building of the Teanlowe centre in 1968.

An unusual entry in the parish registers relates to James Standen Whiteside. Born in Poulton, he was a merchant living in St Pierre on the island of Martinique and in 1800, at the age of only twenty-eight,

Renting pews was a useful way of raising money for the upkeep of the church. Brass plates indicated the owners.

he made a will in which he had a particular request: 'That the megro boy Poulton should have his Liberty, in consideration of his having acted as a True and faithful Servant during my life and should he have an Inclination of going to Europe, You will be good enough to send him by the first opportunity to Mrs James Hull, Poulton in Fylde.' Whiteside died in 1802 and on 26 January 1803 the following entry appears in St Chad's baptismal register: 'James Paulson a negro boy apparently about twelve years of age, lately the property of Standen Whiteside of the island of Martinique, merchant deceased, and to whom by will he gave him his freedom as reward for faithful service.'

One of the methods for raising money to pay for the re-ordering of the church in 1751 was to rent pews to church goers. Families then had a brass name plate screwed to the door of their pew and it was recognised by all that those pews were not to be used by others. The practice brought in a reasonable income which gradually increased over the years, the money being put towards major projects such as the hot water apparatus installed the church in 1856 at a cost of £92, and rent from certain pews was put towards the organist's salary. However the system of renting pews could lead to discord. Mr Gaulter and Mr Bennett put in a complaint against the church wardens who had assigned the pew in the south gallery recently occupied by Mrs Gaulter to Mr James Richardson rather than Mr Bennett who had applied for it. Mr Richardson had a large family and had been waiting over five years. Mr Bennett said he would continue to occupy the pew till he was turned out by force. Others sub-let their pews and never attended St Chad's at all, pews were treated as possessions and bequeathed from one generation to the next; in 1839 George Lewtas left two pews – one in the north gallery 'now occupied by Robert Simpson' and one in the west gallery 'now occupied by Henry Riding' – to his grandchildren. By the early twentieth century the difficulties caused by pew renters not attending church services with their pews remaining empty while others could find no room had become untenable. In 1914 the vicar was anticipating a difficult meeting at which this was to be discussed, drawing up two pages of pencilled notes to persuade the parishioners to call an end to the system of renting pews. In the event the meeting passed off satisfactorily with a large majority voting in favour of change. People had made themselves comfortable in their personal pews and had to be reminded to remove their books, mats and carpets. The system ended after a period of over 170 years, but several of the pews both on the ground floor and in the galleries still carry brass plates with the names of the original benefactors.

CHAPTER 11

The Fleetwood Connection

There are several painted panels in St Chad's as there are in many churches of the eighteenth century. These include a painting of the coat of arms of the monarch, a tradition imposed by statute by Charles II after the Restoration, and six hatchments. A hatchment is the representation of the 'achievement' of a medieval knight, consisting of the shield, helm and other items that were carried at his funeral. When a member of a

Hatchments from the Fleetwood family, of which six hang in St Chad's.

The dovecote at Mains Hall. The house has long associations with Poulton families, particularly the Allens and the Heskeths. It is now open to the public as a hotel and restaurant.

Rossall Hall the family home of the Allens and later Sir Peter Fleetwood Hesketh, who insisted that when he left it should become a school.

local gentry family died a painted hatchment was hung outside the house during the period of mourning and afterwards in the parish church. These diamond-shaped paintings are often to be seen hanging on the walls of Georgian churches, a tradition originally from the Low Countries but popular in England from the seventeenth until the early nineteenth centuries. Hatchments in Lancashire date mainly from the eighteenth and nineteenth centuries. Those in St Chad's are memorials of various members of the Fleetwood and related families. The manor and advowson (i.e. the right of recommending a member of the clergy for a vacant position) of Poulton were claimed by the crown at the Reformation and St Chad's passed to John Fleetwood, lord of the manor of Penwortham and his descendants were to remain patrons of the living until 1935.

At some time, possibly the re-ordering of the mid 1880s, it was decided to remove the hatchments from the walls and store them in the belfry. In 1909 they were restored and put back in the church but this resulted in them acquiring a discolouration so dark that by the 1990s it was difficult to pick out the details. Pat Allois has recently restored them to their original condition they now provide a splash of colour against the whitewashed walls.

At the back of St Chad's next to the south door is one panel from the family pew of the Fleetwoods in which is set a door from the Rigby pew. Family pews allowed members of local gentry families to attend church but kept them separate from the mass of the congregation. The pews are all of similar design – a solid panel to a height of about four feet with a series of open panels on top which allowed those seated inside to see the

Sir Peter Fleetwood Hesketh.

A Medieval illustration showing a farmed rabbit warren. Fleetwood was built on land once used as a warren.

The door to the Fleetwood family vault with an inscription over the door dated 1699.

preacher and the choir in the west gallery, but prevented anyone seeing them. The familiar three-decker pulpit of the time was necessary so the preacher was raised up high enough to be seen through these open panels. These family pews were usually situated in a prime position close to the

Part of the Fleetwood family pew was moved in 1886 to become a wall of the baptistry in the south west corner of the church.

chancel and many had a separate door that allowed the family to enter the pew without passing through the church itself. In St Chad's the Fleetwood pew stood where the choir stalls are now, the door a few feet away, allowed private access. Some pews were extremely comfortable, with green baize seats, cushions and even fireplaces. A brick-lined vault lies beneath the choirstalls, where members of the Fleetwood family were buried from 1699 to the mid-nineteenth century.

In 1888 when the Revd J. Richardson died and the parishioners wanted his son the Revd E.P. Richardson to follow him, Mrs Charles Hesketh, the patron of St Chad's, considered him too young and appointed the Revd Thomas Hill Guest, much to the disappointment of the parishioners who raised a petition signed by thirty people but to no avail. In 1925 Major Fleetwood Hesketh decided not to pass on the inherited right to appoint vicars of Poulton to his heirs. His decision was not made public but came to light in 1933 when a new Act of Parliament came into force regarding the purchase of rights of patronage. The advowson of St Chad's passed to the Diocese of Blackburn in 1934 when, at a well attended meeting, a price of £600 was agreed. The Fleetwood family had appointed vicars at Poulton for 400 years.

Two of the most influential Poulton families during the eighteenth and nineteenth centuries were the Thornbers and the Harrisons. Giles Thornber and Elizabeth Harrison had four sons and a daughter surviving to adulthood, all remembered in family memorials in St Chad's churchyard. Giles Thornber was a magistrate and took part in the first meeting of the county court held in Poulton in 1847. In 1818 he had been a member of the select committee that considered plans for the building of the first church in Blackpool. In 1837 William Thornber's book *A History of Blackpool and its Neighbourhood* was printed by Arthur Smith at his works on the west side of the Market Place in Poulton, now the site of a bank. William derived a life long interest in local history from his mother Elizabeth Harrison herself descended from an old Fylde family. Another branch of the Harrisons is commemorated on a large memorial stone which stands at the bottom of the gallery staircase in St Chad's church. In the early years of the nineteenth century Elizabeth Harrison's uncle, Edward Harrison MD, moved from Poulton to Horncastle in Lincolnshire where he became a family physician to two major figures of the day, Alfred Lord Tennyson and Sir Joseph Banks, the explorer and botanist.

William Thornber 1803-1885. The author of an early history of Blackpool, William came from an old Poulton family.

CHAPTER 12

Travelling to Poulton

In the sixteenth and seventeenth centuries the upkeep of local roads had to be paid for by the inhabitants in labour and cash. Poulton's roads, like many others, were often in poor condition and over the years increasing traffic made the problem worse. Highways Surveyors was responsible for setting a rate and collecting the money from reluctant inhabitants. When Thomas Dobson held the post he requested the JPs to force people to pay the rate but actually paid for some of the stone himself. A big issue was the bridge over the River Wyre at Skippool, carrying the main road from Poulton to Preston and to Garstang. In 1634 a petition from leading inhabitants of Poulton requested that money should be collected to pay – yet again – for the rebuilding of the bridge which was 'in very great decay to the general hindrance and prejudice of all'. Several carts and carriages had actually fallen through the decayed bridge. Each rebuild had been in wood, as sufficient money was never available for it to be built in stone. In a countrywide report to Commissioners in 1649 regarding the state of the country's churches the inhabitants of Marton made a case for them to be detached from the parish of Poulton and form a new parish citing the state of the roads as their main reason. 'The township of Marton within the said parish, by distance from Poulton five miles and no nearer to any other church or chapel, the inhabitants in the winter season being for the most

Travel on nineteenth-century roads was often difficult and uncomfortable. This old coach from that period was left to decay in a local garden.

part debarred from any church or chapel by water and being a great number of families, they humbly desire that they may be made a parish and that Laiton, Raikes and Blackpoole, being hamlets near adjoining, may be annexed to them and that a church or chapel may be erected and a minister and competent maintenance allowed.'

Properly made roads were a rarity until the establishment of the stage coach in the late eighteenth century. Arthur Young wrote a description in 1770 of the main road running from Wigan to Preston and on to Lancaster, warning travellers: 'I know not in the whole language, terms sufficiently expressive to describe this infernal road. Let me caution travellers to avoid it as they would the devil, for a thousand to one but they break their necks or their limbs by overthrows or breaking downs. They will meet with ruts, which I actually measured four feet deep, and floating with mud only from a wet summer. What therefore must it be after a winter? The only mending it receives is a tumbling in of some loose stones which serve no other purpose but jolting the carriage in the most intolerable manner. I actually passed three carts broken down in this 18 miles of execrable memory.' Frances Bold on her way to Rossall Hall after her marriage to Fleetwood Hesketh in 1759 had to travel by horseback, accompanied by her bridesmaids, the roads being too bad to take carriage wheels.

Stage coaches appear to have started services in the Fylde on 1 August 1780 with a coach running on Mondays and Wednesdays from Manchester to Bolton, Chorley and Blackburn extended to include Blackpool. The journey from Manchester to Blackpool took the whole day starting at 6 a.m. and the inside fare was 14s. A service from Halifax to Blackpool began in 1782. The larger houses and farms were converted into coffee houses or inns and four new purpose-built inns were built, forming the beginning of Blackpool's role as a major seaside resort. In the late eighteenth century Blackpool overflowed with visitors who, finding no accommodation in the town, were obliged to find lodgings in Poulton, spending their days on the sands and returning to Poulton in the evening.

Coaches from Preston to Blackpool came up the Breck to the Black Bull inn. In summer both visitors to Blackpool and the mail came by this route and in winter the mail came by post boy on horseback. There is little record of the early postal service for Poulton although in 1669 a foot messenger was advertised as travelling between Preston and Kirkham once or twice a week. The growth of Blackpool as a bathing resort also improved Poulton's facilities. A delivery link between Preston, Kirkham and Poulton was established and George Cook, the first postmaster in Blackpool, received mail from Poulton. In 1807, late deliveries of Poulton mail led over sixty of the principal inhabitants of Poulton to send a petition to the two Postmasters General, requesting a regular postal service from Garstang. This was refused but pressure eventually led to the establishment of the Penny

The Black Bull hotel was a popular stopping place for coaches and charabancs. Notice the opening hours displayed over the bank next door in this scene from around 1900.

Post in the Fylde with Preston as head office. Unfortunately some mail now went to the village of Poulton near Lancaster! After consultation with Paul Thornber, the Clerk to the Magistrates, it was decided to rename the town Poulton-le Fylde, which was eventually done in 1842.

In 1722 Poulton was part of the Port of Chester. Although the local port was at Skippool there was constant danger of flooding there so customs and the commercial centre was at Poulton where, in the reign of Queen Anne, the customs officer received £30 per year. The River Wyre was considered much safer than either the Ribble or the Lune and could be entered by vessels in stormy weather. The 'bottle-neck' estuary was recognised early as a suitable harbour for shipping, 'safe and easy as Wyre water.' But seafaring

The River Wyre looking across to Wardleys.

The market cross, stocks, fish slab and whipping post.

Mesolithic elk found in Carleton, now in the Harris Museum, Preston.

During the 1570s Christopher Saxton published the first county maps of England. This is the Fylde.

This vestment belongs to St John's Catholic church. It has been dated to the late fifteenth century and may have been in use at St Chad's before the Reformation.

A view over the roof of the Golden Ball towards the River Wyre.

The war memorial was moved from its original site in Queens Square in the 1970s.

St Chad's parish church was first recorded in 1094.

Interior of St Chad's from the chancel steps.

The coat of arms of George III in St Chad's.

The Thatched House in Chapel Street with the original Ship Inn in the distance.

A typical site for a pub is at the entrance to an old churchyard.

Smaller properties line Ball Street.

Victoria Road runs off the Breck.

One of the properties built on the Breck.

The Stocks, now a restaurant. In the 1840s this was the home of Thomas Hulton, a surgeon.

The Spread Eagle Inn on the left was one of Poulton's coaching inns.

Potts Alley transformed into Chapel Street Court with coffee shops and restaurants.

Three of the oldest properties remaining in Poulton, the far one probably dating from the seventeenth century.

The Civic Centre, originally built as a convalescent home, later became a teacher training college.

The River Wyre hotel at the bottom of the Breck. The building in the distance was the original pub.

The ancient stocks and market cross contrast with the modern Bull hotel.

This property has been a shop for several generations but retains much of its original shape and character above street level.

The Old Town Hall was originally the Bay Horse. It became the offices of Poulton Urban District Council before reverting to its former role in the 1980s.

The Breck became a popular position for new homes in the 1880s.

The Park was developed on original glebe land between Vicarage Road and the Green.

The Golden Ball, once the town's reading room.

Little Poulton Hall built around 1750. It replaced a much older house occupied by the Heskeths from the mid-sixteenth century, and later the Fitzherbert Brockholes.

The churchyard is carpeted by crocus in early spring.

from the Wyre was not always safe. Thus on 20 August 1826 Captain Wilding with two others and a cabin boy were returning to Liverpool from Poulton and as they left the River Wyre in an open boat they were beaten by a heavy gale and sunk with the loss of all lives.

On the far side of the river Wyre was a second port, Wardleys. In 1831 the *Hope*, a ship of 450 tons built by William Lewtas at Wardleys, was launched and crowds came from all over the district only to be drenched as it went into the water and flooded Skippool Road. The tidal estuary of the River Wyre reaches as far as St Michaels, 14 miles from its mouth, providing an effective barrier between Over Wyre and Poulton. Ferries had existed at Aldwath, Wardleys and Knott End for centuries but by the 1860s increased agricultural markets led to the building of the Shard Toll Bridge, authorised by a private Act of Parliament. The bridge opened in 1864 and although a report in 1949 recommended a new crossing it was not until 1992 that a new free bridge replaced the original.

By the eighteenth century Lancaster had developed as a major centre for commerce and work on Glasson, a small port nearer the mouth of the Lune, was completed in 1791. Some years later a branch of the Lancaster Canal was opened to Glasson, enabling goods to be transported by water straight to Preston. It had been proposed that a branch of the Lancaster Canal should be built to link Poulton and Kirkham and improve their trading facilities, but nothing came of the suggestion. Trade at both Skippool and Glasson was badly affected when Sir Peter Fleetwood Hesketh put forward plans in 1830 to build a new port nearer to the sea than both Skippool and Wardleys. As High Sheriff of Lancashire he had attended the opening of the Liverpool-Manchester railway in 1830 and it was possibly this event which gave him the idea of founding a new town on his estate at Rossall which

An aerial view of two Shard bridges over the River Wyre, the new one complete and the original about to be demolished in 1992.

Skippool was once a busy port and is now a haven for sailing.

could be linked by rail to Preston and beyond.

In 1831 an extension of the Wigan branch of the Liverpool and Manchester railway ran to Preston and in 1835 the Preston and Wyre Harbour and Dock Company obtained Parliamentary powers to construct a railway from the terminus of the North Union Railway in Preston to Fleetwood. A harbour and docks were established from which a service of steamers could be run to Scotland and Ireland. The Preston-Fleetwood railway line was opened on 15 July 1840 linking the Fylde with Preston and Manchester and bringing the important Preston market within reach of the large number of farms in the Fylde for the sale of their produce.

The completion of the planned town of Fleetwood, designed by the architect Decimus Burton, put paid to Poulton's importance as a port.

The North Euston Hotel in Fleetwood, as its name implies, was built at the northern end of this railway from London.

The Muskpratt *at Skippool bringing grain for the Parkinson Tomlinson mill in Poulton.*

Skippool could no longer compete with the facilities for ocean traffic now afforded by Fleetwood and Poulton's commerce declined. The town finally lost its role when the work of the customs house was transferred to Fleetwood in 1839. However as early as 1788 a visitor to Blackpool had commented that Poulton 'was once a port of some eminence, but is now a small town on the decline consisting of seven sleepy streets'. During the industrialisation of England in the nineteenth century, market towns such as Poulton developed at a much slower rate than their industrial neighbours just as towns connected to the railway network usually grew faster as trade links improved. The population of Poulton remained very stable until the turn of the twentieth century when the first signs of the present-day trend towards growth became apparent.

In the late sixteenth century the trade from Skippool had consisted mainly of tallow, flax and hemp. Ships were laden with timber from America, grain from Scotland and tallow and flax from Russia. Later there sprang up trade in cotton, corn timber and flax from Belfast which was shipped to many points abroad. The importing of flax and hemp from Belfast via Poulton gave rise to the manufacture of sail-cloth and cordage, coarse and fine linen and some cotton. Rope making required a 'rope walk' – a long narrow building in which the twisted yarns could be made into rope. A 600ft rope required a path 1,000ft long. The site of the Poulton ropewalk is still recognisable in the line of the modern Stanley Avenue. In 1846 Robert Hornby Porter noted 'the rope works in Sandy Lane are doing well'.

CHAPTER 13

A Town of Shopkeepers

Following the Market Place fire in 1732 which demolished the whole of the west side, the rebuilding was done as a block with a uniformity of size, frontage and roof line still obvious today. However it is possible the block was erected to a new building line further to the east making the Market Place slightly narrower. The Bull pub now actually faces the end of the buildings on the west side. If the original buildings prior to the 1732 rebuild had been set further back as is suggested, the original Black Bull inn would have had a clear view across the Market Place and would also have been clearly visible to those seeking a drink. In 1837 William Thornber described the streets of Poulton as 'unpaved, the inhabitants holding connexion with each other's dwellings by stepping stones: the extent of the first essay at making a decent road is still known by the name of the New Pavement.' Thornber then gives an account of the burning down of the property in the Market Place; it is possible that the laying down of the New Pavement and the rebuild of the Market Place were part of the modernisation of the town centre in the late 1730s.

However, it is obvious that the south end of the new block has a different roof line and general appearance and would therefore appear to

A view of the Market Place in the 1920s showing the suggested line of the 'New Pavement'.

Two of William Smith's motor buses wait for passengers by the Market Cross in around 1920. Richards' shop on the corner appears to be a later addition to the new line of buildings constructed after the fire of 1732.

have been added slightly later. The origins of Richards' shop, which became one of the best-known businesses in Poulton is thought to go back to 1754. Traces of the eighteenth century could be seen in the shop, in the form of solid rough-hewn beams in the ceiling, three-foot thick walls and a stone-flagged floor. The business's foundations were laid by Mr John Hodgson, an ironmonger and grocer. By 1828 Thomas Wilding was trading there as a baker and dealer in flour and at the same time running a business as a rope and twine maker and flax dresser, probably making use of the large house across the road on Bull Street which had once belonged to Sir Alexander Rigby. By 1841 Robert Dunderdale from Garstang had taken over the shop as an ironmonger's. Dunderdale had been apprenticed as a youth to John Threlfall an ironmonger in Darwen Street Blackburn and had moved to Poulton in 1834. Nail making was an important business in Poulton with a warehouse in operation on the site of Burlington Avenue, now the Teanlowe Centre, until machine-made nails from Birmingham took away the trade. In 1861 a young man of twenty-two, named Thomas Worthington, joined the business and eight years later took over the ironmonger's shop. Shortly before the first of the Richards family took it over in 1895 the grocery business was finally closed and the ironmongery side expanded to include agricultural machinery as well as tinware. The first of the Richards family, Mr Ebenezer Richards, took over the business in 1895. Richards finally closed in the late 1960s.

Robert Dunderdale remained at the corner ironmonger's shop for nearly thirty years before moving in 1869 to live at a house near the corner of Queens Square and Sheaf Street, where he continued in business as a timber merchant in partnership with Frederick Kemp in the New Fylde Timber Company, also serving as a JP. Dunderdale was something of a property speculator, building a house against all advice at South Shore, an area of sand dunes as yet undeveloped, and later houses in Clifton Street, Blackpool. In the early years of the nineteenth century his house in Queens Square had been the home of Mr Harrison, owner of a business manufacturing sacking, sail cloth and sheeting and employing thirty or forty people in weaving sheds situated behind the house. The property was later used as the Poulton workhouse and small looms were installed in the weaving sheds to give employment to the poor who came there. Queens Square was known as Workhouse Square until Queen Victoria's accession in 1837.

In later years the idea of useful employment in the workhouse was overturned and they became places to dump the poor. The purpose-built workhouses of the nineteenth century aimed to deter people from going there by having in place a system of hard labour. The last governor of Poulton workhouse was John Staning. In 1837 the workhouse function for Poulton was transferred to the new purpose-built workhouse in Kirkham, which became the centre of the Fylde Poor Law Union of twenty-three townships including Poulton. There is no record of the building in Poulton being sold off, suggesting that it had probably been leased for the purpose. Out relief was abolished and there are no longer records in the Poulton vestry minutes as decisions regarding the poor were now being made at Kirkham. Poulton had a lot less influence on what happened to the poor in its own township and the responsibilities of the vestry meeting in this regard came to an end.

Queens Square with a cobbled surface and a new gas lamp on the corner property. This was Workhouse Square until Victoria's coronation in 1837.

CHAPTER 14

The Railway

When the rail link was set up between Preston and Fleetwood in 1840 Poulton was fortunate to lie on the direct line between Kirkham and Fleetwood and the railway station built on a site at the bottom of the Breck was conveniently placed to bring financial gain to the town and to those whose land it crossed. Markets for cattle and cloth were held in Poulton three times a year with a weekly fair on Mondays. Goods for the fairs came in through the ports at Skippool and Wardleys and by rail. In 1847 a fortnightly cattle fair was introduced, supplied by Irish and Scottish dealers through Fleetwood. Tradesmen recognised the value of the site and businesses grew up round the new railway station. The three coal merchants whose businesses were based at the station also dealt in slate, flags, lime and horse and bone manure. The gasworks opened in Station Road in 1851.

For the first few years the railway brought visitors to the town on their way to the developing seaside resort of Blackpool, as they alighted from the train in Poulton to be taken on to Blackpool by horse-drawn charabancs or omnibuses. On occasions the number of passengers from the trains exceeded the seats on the omnibus and wagonettes had to be brought into use. Fleetwood itself developed at first as a successful holiday resort and in 1844 and the Preston and Wyre Railway Company became one of the first to run cheap excursions to the seaside on

The original station ran across the road at the bottom of the Breck. There is now virtually no trace of it left.

Charabancs similar to this took passengers from Poulton station to Blackpool before the rail link was built.

Sundays during the summer months, a service which proved to be remarkably successful. One group consisted of over 2,300 members of a Sunday school travelling in twenty-seven open carriages 'studded with numerous colours and bearing appropriate mottoes'. During the half-hour stay in Poulton station 'the whole multitude were engaged in singing hymns'. In 1846 a link line to Blackpool was opened with a design fault which was to prove fatal half a century later.

In September 1847 Victoria and Albert, with the Prince of Wales, were returning from a holiday in Scotland and had travelled from Ardrossan in the Royal Yacht to Fleetwood where a crowd of about 10,000 awaited them. The children of Poulton were given the day off – a very rare event – and they took their places in the coal trucks belonging to William Catterall, which gave them a good view close to the line as the train passed through Poulton station on its way to Preston and on to London.

By 1852 four trains a day each way were running between Manchester and Blackpool and one each way on Sundays. Only one of these trains carried third-class passengers – the rest catered for first and second class only. It was then fashionable to cater for the nobility and gentry and at that time there was little provision for the crowds who would become Blackpool's main livelihood. Traffic grew on the route through Poulton to Blackpool and Fleetwood and in 1888 the Preston and Wyre railway which had run the line from its beginning in 1840 was taken over by a joint committee of the LNWR and L&YR. The line was doubled and in some places quadrupled to carry the extra traffic and a new station was built at Kirkham. But at Poulton there was a dangerously tight curve close to the level crossing carrying the line across the Breck. Under an Act of Parliament of 1892 powers had already been obtained for a new

A fatal rail crash occurred when a driver took a tight bend at Poulton too fast in 1893.

station on another site, a project local people had long pressed for, and plans were in place to realign the rails and build a new station at the top of the Breck.

On the evening of 1 July 1893 Mr Sutton was preparing for bed when he heard the sound of a train travelling too fast on the line between Blackpool and Poulton station which ran close to his house. Disturbed by the speed of the train he jumped out of bed and opened a window overlooking the line; the train had already passed but about half a minute later he heard the crash. The 11 p.m. train from Blackpool to Stockport, carrying about fifty passengers, had taken the curve too fast and derailed. The engine and carriages ran on a further 40 yards before they overturned, blocking the lines to Fleetwood. Two passengers and the driver were killed and forty-two passengers suffered injuries. The injured were taken to the nearby Railway and Station Hotel while the Royal Oak across the road served as a mortuary. An inquiry agreed that the driver, thirty-eight-year-old Cornelius Ridgeway, was unfamiliar with the track and either failed to see the warning signals or recognise the dangers ahead. The fireman giving evidence at the inquiry said that he and Ridgeway had spent the day in Blackpool and had 'nothing to drink but three glasses of beer each'. The report continued, 'There was not the least reason for suspicion on the part of those who had seen Ridgeway and Lowe before the train left Blackpool that either of them was at all under the influence of liquor.'

Tenders for the work on the new station were put out in March 1894 and the project was awarded to Messrs Edward Taylor & Co. of Littleborough. The old station at the bottom of the Breck was to become the goods station. Before building could begin land and buildings had to be bought from about forty owners near the route of the new railway line. In Tithebarn Street four cottages were demolished, one house in Breck Road, two cottages across the road from Mr Sykes and two houses on the south side of the new line belonging to Mr Raby. Two houses close by belonging to Mr J. Jackson were also purchased; one was used as an engineer's house but in the end both were left standing. In March 1923 Poulton Curve station was built and remained in use until 29 November 1952. Almost alongside the curve station ran an ancient watercourse known as Horsebridge Dyke and during the 1990s the whole area was turned into a park incorporating the disused railway line, now a haven for wildlife, and the watercourse.

The line of the original railway track can be seen in this 1930 photograph. The large building was built as a convalescent home, became a teacher training college and is now Wyre Civic Centre.

CHAPTER 15

Health, Schools and the Poor

In many ways the development of Poulton has been the result of development going on around it rather than by any planning on its own part. In 1837 it was famously described as 'the metropolis of the Fylde.' But in spite of having the railway, a port, a safe river, a weekly market, three annual fairs and four 'hotels', Poulton did not develop into a new industrial town as did Kirkham. In fact one writer commented in the 1870s, 'The fairs which some years ago were of considerable local importance are now mere nonentities from a business point of view and unless some enterprising manufacturer builds either workshop or factory in the neighbourhood, the town generally promises fair to follow in their wake.' The linen industry was widespread in the area in the eighteenth century but in spite of substantial imports of flax and goods warehouses at Skippool, it was the Birleys, the Langtons and the Hornbys – merchants from Kirkham – who ran the trade. These included, ironically, John Birley, originally a Poulton man who had married into a flax merchant family and settled in Kirkham. In 1795 the production of coarse linens and sailcloth was the chief trade of that town. Poulton's relative isolation from the coalfields and sources of cheap labour and a lack of facilities for transporting goods to and from the interior of the county, combined to determine the town's future: it was not to be one of industrial development. Looking back from the distance of the

A horse fair in the early twentieth century. The last fair took place in 1927.

International fashions
were made available
for Poulton ladies by
bonnet makers like
the Crookall sisters.

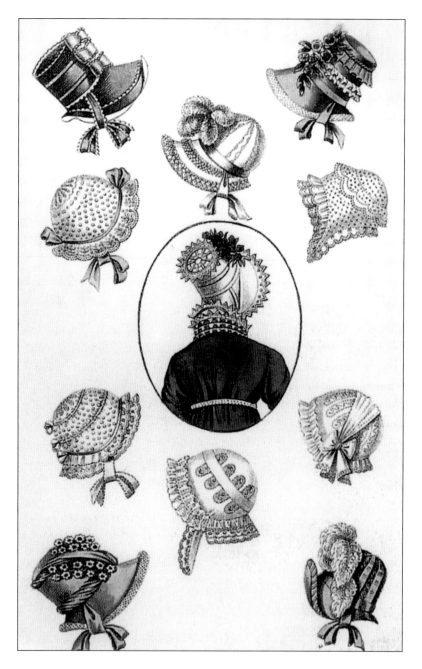

twenty-first century some may now be pleased that Poulton took the
course it did.

A request for information about the cost of living in Poulton printed
in the *Monthly Magazine* in August 1816 drew the following information
from an inhabitant of the town. The best flour was selling at 56s per
pack, butter at 10d for 20oz; however, during the summer season the
price of butter went up a penny due to the proximity of Blackpool. Eggs

were 6d per dozen, milk 2d a quart, beef 6d a pound, veal 4½d, and other local produce equally reasonable in price. Rents were low but there was little property available. A hint of dissatisfaction with unruly behaviour in the town crept in as the writer commented 'I can say little in favour of the good regulations of the town, there being no Justice of the Peace for about 18 miles'. However his final comment was very positive – the correspondent 'would find no difficulty in being able to live in Poulton in a small establishment, with respectability, for less than £100 a year' The nearby village of Blackpool, rapidly finding popularity with visitors, still relied on the market at Poulton to provide its daily requirements.

The difficulties of making a living in Poulton are recorded in a letter sent on 24 April 1843 to John Thornber from his solicitor Alexander Liddell. It appears that Thornber had let his house in Tithebarn Street to two sisters, Grace and Ellen Crookall who were bonnet makers. Their father Ralph Crookall visited Liddell on their behalf with the sad tale that as they could not make a living in Poulton they had shut up the house leaving their father to pay the rent they owed. Liddell commented 'Poulton is wretchedly dull'. An article in the *Preston Guardian* of 1875 suggests that nothing changed: 'Little trade is going on ordinarily in this respectable old town. On the market day the square and streets may present a more lively scene but on the fine August afternoon when the writer visited Poulton for the first time the place wore an air of slumberous stillness undisturbed by wheeled vehicle or by the passage of more than a solitary pedestrian at intervals of a half hour or so. A town like Poulton may afford the visitor a conception of what an average market town in Lancashire was like two or three centuries back.'

For centuries all communities enjoyed a variety of entertainments throughout the year in the way of festivals and ancient traditions which

The maypole symbolises centuries of traditional celebrations in towns like Poulton.

The Market Place is host to one of the many celebrations and entertainments it has seen over the years. This is Club Day in the 1920s.

had been kept up for generations. Both the churchyard and St Chad's were used for events and regular festivals were held at midsummer, Whitsuntide and Michaelmas. But by the mid-nineteenth century the traditional festivities, many of them dating back centuries, were fast disappearing or forgotten. Teanlay Night gave its name to the Teanlowe shopping centre built in Poulton in 1968 after a competition was held to find a name. Originally Teanlay night was the vigil of All Souls when bonfires were lit on hills and mosses across the Fylde and revels held for souls in purgatory. A field named 'Purgatory', near Westfield Avenue in Poulton, was such a site for All Souls, its name simply meaning that it was a difficult field to cultivate.

On Shrove Tuesday morning the pancake bell rang, originally to signal to apprentices that they were entitled to take a holiday for the rest of the day. In the 1830s there were over thirty apprentices in Poulton all supported by money from James Baines' charity but fifty years later there were none. 'Shrove' derives from the Old English word 'shrive' meaning to confess all sins and people would confess in response to the bell which was rung in every parish. However, coming before a forty-day period of austerity, during the Middle Ages Shrove Tuesday was second only to Christmas in its dedication to fun and frivolity. At

A Poulton Festival or Club Day procession of the early 1900s.

the sound of the shriving bell, shops would close and a great feast would take place. Pancakes were made because eggs and fat, forbidden during Lent, needed to be eaten prior to the fast.

May Day saw the streets of Poulton strewn with flowers. Sweetmeats, ale and wine were handed out to those who knocked on doors and a May King and Queen were paraded round the town. The completion of the harvest and other similar milestones in the farming year were times for the whole neighbourhood to celebrate often marked with parades of horse-drawn carts through the streets. At Christmas there were visits from carol singers, mince pies, games of cards and other pastimes whose names are recorded but whose details have vanished. Christmas Eve was 'Flesh Day' when people from outlying communities flocked to Poulton to stock up with beef and other meats and three rows of stalls filled the Market Place from end to end to satisfy the demand.

The annual Easter Monday fair, Whitsuntide sports on the Green and a wide variety of festivities, games and traditional activities throughout the year had in previous times kept the younger generation occupied, but by the mid nineteenth century many of the familiar neighbourhood traditions were dying out and Poulton centre, with its pubs and beer sellers, saw more and more groups collecting after work, getting drunk, showering insults on passers-by and resorting to crime. In 1805 things had become so bad that 'articles of agreement' were dawn up and signed by over a hundred gentlemen of Poulton stating that they would share the costs of prosecuting wrong doers, 'so that the inhabitants of Poulton may have all the possible comforts of a peaceable neighbourhood.' Crimes included the 'stealing of fuel, poultry and other things, robbing orchards and gardens, maiming and abusing cattle and many mischievous things that can't be classified under any general heading.'

The County Police Act had seen the formation of the Lancashire Constabulary. Poulton now had a resident police constable and also provided a base for a police inspector. In 1837 an experiment saw two deputy constables on duty on Saturday and Sunday evenings for a fortnight. In October that year it was agreed that 'the peace of the town be maintained by putting the constables on duty when needful.' On 23 April 1839 Giles Thornber proposed to the vestry meeting that there should be a town lockup 'for the good and safety of the town'. A public meeting was arranged to discuss it and members of the vestry were ordered to look out for a suitable building. It was not until the following year that a lockup was proposed in buildings belonging to Mr Kemp, and another public meeting held to discuss this the following month at George Hardman's house, presumably the Thatched where he was landlord. At yet another vestry meeting it was decided that a property belonging to John Thornton, the landlord of the Black Bull, would be suitable and would be let for the purpose at a rate of £9 per annum. In 1842 legislation concerning the appointment and payment of parish constables was introduced and a list of twenty men nominated to be constables in Poulton was sent to the magistrates.

Following the introduction of legislation in the early nineteenth century a group of twenty inhabitants elected from those eligible to pay the poor rate tax formed the 'Select Vestry' and acted as a sort of local council, a development from the 'four and twenty men' of the 1630s. In a small community like Poulton it was essential that these should be men who were educated and respected by the community in general in order to administer the distribution of poor relief without accusation of bias and irregularity. Although under legislation not strictly its role, the Select Vestry also took responsibility for public health, highways and law and order. In Poulton the Overseers of the Poor were chosen by a Magistrate from a list of ten or so whose names were put forward.

Each year Poulton Select Vestry met to decide on the rate for the following year. Under poor law legislation individuals were assessed for Poor Rate through valuations made on their land and buildings, goods and tithes and the final rateable value was based on the rent which could be asked for the property.

The Vestry met fortnightly in the workhouse and considered a wide variety of requests mainly for temporary relief for emergencies such as sickness or debt. Betty Eaves applied for potatoes for sets; she was allowed one load of potatoes 'on condition her husband parting with a dog kept by him'. Alice Holland applied by letter for casual relief on the grounds of sickness and the Overseers of Poulton wrote to the officers in Walton, presumably where she had come from, to check whether it was genuine – they replied that it was but that she was 'not likely to continue long'. A typical case is that of a letter from the Overseer for Preston explaining that the wife and children of William Brade were chargeable to Poulton – he was in prison for debt. Thomas Ibbitson had told the Overseers he was the beneficiary of a will and was waiting for his payment and in the meantime was applying for relief. The Overseers were dubious and stopped his weekly payment of 3s; presumably they felt Thomas should be looking for work rather than living off the poor rate.

Some were granted long-term relief – those with chronic illness, the elderly, the feeble, invalids and their dependents and orphans. Help with items such as furniture and trade equipment could be provided. The Vestry would also deal with apprenticeships, and liaise with other townships over paupers. Unmarried mothers frequently applied for support. Betty Bond was concerned for her five-week-old baby whose father Benjamin Hall was now living with his brother Richard in Garstang. In order to get him to pay for the support of the child an application would have to be made to the Quarter Sessions which would be expensive. The overseers were asked to write and request him to come to an arrangement with the mother. Benjamin refused and an application was made for an order of maintenance to be heard at the Quarter Sessions. Alice Hull applied to go into the workhouse while she had her baby – the request was refused. Kirkham Overseers requested money for clothing for two children from Poulton now living in Kirkham – also refused. 30s was paid towards the funeral costs for Nanny Clarkson. William Porter, a pauper in the Workhouse, was to have his visit to a doctor in Manchester for treatment for his diseased leg. William Brindle was allowed 9s for a visit to Preston. John Adcock applied for something in order to enable him to bury his wife 'who died this day'. A sum of £2 and a new suit of clothes were given to Robert Roe for his new apprentice Adam Kellett. The Overseers were even involved in valuing land and properties taken for building the new railway. The house of the Revd Porter was valued at £10 and the house and outbuildings of William Crane in Tithbarn Street at £6.

Much of the responsibility lay in balancing provision for those of the parish in trouble with careful budgeting of the public money collected through taxes, typified by the case of William Hartley, when the assistant overseer had to see that he has proper surgical assistance from the surgeon now attending him' but that he should also 'use all expedition in throwing the burden of Hartley's maintenance on the Township to which he belongs'. The system relied on those eligible paying their share and this was not easy to enforce. The Overseer reported the names of such persons as refused or neglected payment to a special meeting of the Vestry.

Chapel Street, with the Ship Inn in the distance in the early 1900s.

The role of the Vestry widened even further as they took on the scrutiny of the roads and sewerage. Concern about public health had been growing nationally particularly because of the recurring epidemics of cholera. In 1826 an epidemic of cholera broke out in Poulton with twenty-one people contracting the disease; nine of those living on Breck Street died. People were becoming more aware and more fastidious, less willing to put up with smells and rotting rubbish in the streets. In Poulton there was discussion as to whether a Board of Health should be established but it was decided against. The Vestry tried to encourage the inhabitants to clean up the town. In October 1842 Mr Richard Parkinson was requested to make up and repair the spot on the causeway where his weighing machine formerly stood near the top of the Green. Middensteads at properties in Back Street (now Chapel Street) were ordered to be removed – Thomas Walsh was ordered to remove the bones and rags lying in a cellar in Church Street from which offensive smells were issuing and the residents of Potts Lane, now Chapel Street Court, were requested 'immediately to remove the nuisances therein'.

Legislation on public health was not brought in until 1848 and then only applied to large towns. The Vestry had no right to make local bye-laws, only to call the bluff of the offenders. It seems the requests of the Vestry had gone unheeded. On 19 August 1848 a public meeting was held to discuss the problems facing the town. It was agreed to write to all owners of lodging houses in Poulton 'requesting them to take early measures to clear their houses as there was a great danger of disease arising out of their crowded and filthy state.' Having dealt with the most

Church Street. The lodging house on the right housed itinerant workers especially at harvest time and was known as Twenty Steps.

obvious cause of danger to public health a committee was formed to 'examine the nuisances in the town' and report back to a meeting a week later on 25 August.

Tithebarn Street and the Breck were in good order but in Ball Street they found a large open cesspool into which a large wooden open drain discharged its contents. As this was behind a butcher's shop, run by Richard Bond, the instructions were that it required immediate attention. In Back Street there was a pool of stagnant water surrounded by decaying vegetable material and another in The Green. Another drain and cesspool was found near Dudley Hall a small thatched cottage which stood on the site now occupied by Poulton Library. In Wheatsheaf Street all the channels were reported to be in need of replacement. In a passage on the west side of the Market Place they found another large open cesspool and reported that 'it would be very desirable for this to be amended as from its central situation it might become prejudicial to the neighbouring dwellings.'

The horror of the inspection team is palpable as they recorded their reaction to Potts Lane: 'The Potts Lane is in very bad condition from end to end, the smell in front of the houses is very offensive, a little farther are six pigstyes the nuisance from which is very bad. In addition to which they are infected by a number of rats many of which burrow in the churchyard immediately behind and are frequently seen running about even in the daytime. There is also a privy common to the houses having a long passage leading to it. This passage is in an indescribable state. More we cannot say as the first view deterred us from a nearer inspection. A practice which prevails in this row is that of the residents throwing out the contents of their chamber utensils through the back room windows into the churchyard. This seems to have been carried on

for some time and constitutes a most offensive nuisance against health and decency independently of the desecration of the surrounding tombstones and graves which it necessarily involves.' A meeting was held in the Savings Bank in October 1848 to discuss 'the sanitary condition of the town' and continued to meet for some weeks.

A public health inspector's report in the following year also describes horrendous conditions in the town with details that are almost too awful to contemplate. The Golden Ball garden with an open ditch, Richard Parkinson's baker's shop on the Market Place had 'a foul cesspit abutting the street. It is very filthy and the liquid refuse flows into a open channel in the street. Although there is some evidence of this place having been cleaned up for the occasion, it is difficult to imagine anything more disgusting than its state even under these circumstances.' On Tithebarn Street the yard of James Bleasdale and Nicholas Butler who were the carriers between Poulton and Lancaster, was 'flowing with filth and refuse. The open channels in the street adjoining here are all filled with liquid refuse.' Thomason's slaughterhouse and yard was in a wretched condition, the privy at John McManus's lodging house in Church Street was said to be 'always overcharged with excremental matter. Liquid refuse of all kinds is soaking into the surface'. At the back of the Kings Arms inn was another open drain which ran under a house at the end of the row. 'The privies for about a dozen houses near here are all in a most filthy condition.' The back of Breck Street was described as 'very bad with a very offensive open ditch running along its whole length. Privies empty into the ditch. Fever has prevailed in this neighbourhood to a great extent. There are more open and filthy ditches near the railway station.' At the back of the police station was a defective drain that ran under the sitting room floor, the smell from it was 'much complained of'. In 1851 magistrates were requested to put the Lodging House Act into operation in Poulton which it was hoped would go some way towards improving that situation. It was not until 1910 that many of the old buildings causing concern were finally demolished.

Isaac Ismay was born in Blackpool in 1859 and travelled around Lancashire as a hawker, in the early 1880s while living in Skerton near Lancaster. He settled in Poulton in a house on the Green and had his stables in Potts Alley. Given to wearing red and green check shirts, Ike Ismay is remembered as a dealer in all sorts, but he had been horse dealer and would go over to Ireland to bring back stock for the growing market of horse drawn wagonettes, charabancs, cabs and landaus. He trotted horses over the cobbled Market Place for the benefit of prospective buyers often disturbing the peace of a Sunday morning. The narrow streets would be jammed with a variety of horse-drawn vehicles, for many of which Ike Ismay claimed to have provided the horses. The Fylde had become well known for its horses and farmers could get high prices for hunters and coach horses.

One of the many attractions of Poulton on market days was the regulation which allowed the sale of alcohol outside licensing hours provided people had travelled three miles for it. In 1897 Elizabeth Ball, landlady of The Royal Oak pub, was summonsed for serving drink out of hours to William French, stud groom to Mr Miller at Singleton, on 2 September. Superintendent Ormerod said that by the main road the distance from Singleton was 3 miles 341 yards but the nearest road, a private road across the fields, was 64 yards under 3 miles. Mrs Parr, daughter of the landlady at the Railway Hotel, said it had always been the custom to serve people from Singleton without the police interfering. William French had been served many times after hours as he lived over three miles away and Daniel Haslam, Mr Miller's bailiff, said Singleton people had been served for forty years. The case was dismissed.

Stray animals wandering round the narrow streets were a problem and in 1853 the Surveyor of Highways was ordered to provide a suitable pinfold and appoint someone to impound stray cattle found wandering the lanes in the town. It was eventually built on wasteland in Back Lane, now Chapel Street, belonging to George Hardman, a small patch of land lying between the Thatched House and St Chad's. Hardman had claimed damages of £2 but agreed to drop his claim in return for not paying rates for two years. Matters of public health and safety gradually caught the attention of the inhabitants of Poulton. In 1859 a new fire engine was acquired. It was decided that expenses were to be paid out of the highways rates and Thomas Fairclough was given responsibility for

The churchyard became a problem in the late nineteenth century.

The churchyard is crossed by a series of footpaths providing shortcuts through the town centre.

its care, management and repair. Forty years later the condition of Poulton fire brigade's manual engine had deteriorated so much that it was becoming unworkable, with faulty hose pipes so rotten that when they were used the men were almost drowned.

An awareness of the need for protection from illness and disease led to a policy of public vaccination and in September 1863 Dr Stevens, the Government Inspector of vaccination, visited the Sheaf Street School to examine the children's arms and check that the recent vaccinations had taken. He was not happy with his findings and said that many would have to re-vaccinated.

By the middle of the century the graveyard at St Chad's was becoming a public scandal; having been in use for well over a thousand years, it was full. Regularly bones would be removed from the ground and deposited in a charnel house which stood in Potts Alley. In 1805 John Ryding repaired the 'bone house' at a cost of 5s. In 1837 a committee was formed to consider how to prevent the desecration of the churchyard. Rats issuing from the pigsty in Potts Lane and the dogs kept by some of the residents which chased the rats were ravaging the churchyard and concern was expressed that if they continued to run riot they would eventually get into the graves. In order to deal with this grievance it was resolved that the owners of the property should be requested to move pigsties from the church gate, the gate should be locked and the churchyard fenced off. By 1849 the churchyard became so filled with graves as to make it difficult to find places for interments where there was a sufficient depth of soil. In order to stop the burial of people dying out of the parish, an addition to the customary fee was imposed. Again in 1859 a Committee was appointed to consider protection of the burial ground, this time from the children and poultry

Ball Street with the old buildings that lined the churchyard. In the far distance is the Savings Bank.

These youngsters are in the Church of England school in Sheaf Street in around 1900.

trespassing on it. It was agreed that a good thorn fence and a selection of ornamental shrubs be located by the church. The two gates leading to the churchyard from Back Street and Ball Street opposite the Thatched House tavern should be closed and locked every Sunday after the start of the service.

Another report stated that 'On the south side of the church between the chancel door and the south door the accumulation of graves is so great that the ground is raised more than a yard and a half above the level of the remainder of the churchyard and the interments so frequent that it is become impossible to bury so deep as to prevent the obnoxious gas escaping.' The whole matter was made worse by the number of gravestones, some with railings round them which meant there was even less room available for the large number of burials, a problem made worse by the tradition that each parishioner had a right to be buried in the family grave or as near to it as possible. Finally on 30 June 1884 the churchyard was closed for burials. The Burial Board opened a public cemetery in Moorland Road with a chapel at its centre. The chapel was demolished in 1972 and a Garden of Remembrance put in its place and a second cemetery opened on Garstang Road.

In October 1887 Mr Livesey, the Revd Slavan, minister of the Congregational church, and Mr Thomas Hammond, schoolmaster, decided to re-open the library which had been closed for many years in the Savings Bank on the corner of Vicarage Road. It was to be open each Monday, for an hour in the morning and an hour in the evening. Perhaps it was not a success because in 1914 the vicar announced that a large quantity of books belonging to 'a former lending library' in the parish had been stored at the vicarage for many years and were to be sent to the annual jumble sale. Poulton had one of the earliest libraries,

*Cookery class at
Sheaf Street School
around 1900.*

set up by Thomas Bray in the 1690s. Libraries had existed in many parishes in mediaeval times but most were swept away at the Reformation. Although they were usually intended for the use of the clergy, people in the community who could read were able to make use of them. Thomas Bray, born in Shropshire in 1658 and ordained in 1681, was concerned at the lack of Christian teaching in Restoration England and devised a scheme for establishing parochial libraries in deaneries in England and Wales. By the time of his death in 1730 some eighty had been set up in parishes up and down the land, each consisting mostly of standard collections of about seventy volumes. The original books of St Chad's library lay forgotten for years in the church tower and were rediscovered a few years ago. Although the books still belong to St Chad's, they are in the safe keeping of the John Rylands Library in Deansgate, Manchester. A modern version of the Bray Library is still in existence and is run by parishioners.

In the 1840s it was probable that only small proportion of the population of Poulton could read well enough to enjoy reading books for pleasure, although many would have been sufficiently literate and numerate to perform their jobs.

As well as James Baines' free school which was rebuilt in 1828, there were several private schools among them those in Bull Street, Green Street, now Higher Green, and Church Street. Some private schools did well in Poulton remaining in business for many years, others were set up and lasted only a short time. One of the successful schools was opened during the 1850s by Thomas Hammond, a schoolmaster of Sheaf Street who moved into a large property in Ball Street, one of a pair of double-fronted, three-storey houses facing St Chad's. The front entrance to one is still recognisable as such although it is now a shop entrance. The

...

Thomas Hammond set up a school in one of these houses in the nineteenth century. The doorway is still recognisable.

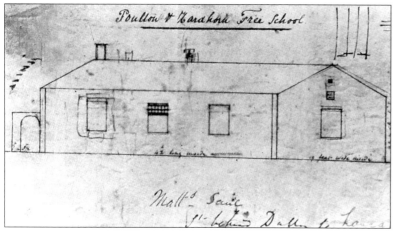

In 1828 plans were prepared for a new building for James Baines' free school.

daughter of Thomas and Jane Hammond, Isabella Ellen, was to become the wife of Sir William Hodgson. In the mid-1870s two more new schools opened, the Church of England School in Sheaf Street which had begun as a Sunday school built by public subscription in 1830, opened as a day school and soon after a Mrs Whiteside opened a school in Staining. This had a profound effect on Poulton Free School which was closed for seven years until in January 1882 when it was reopened, under a new name, 'Baines Endowed School'. This school, a single room built of brick, stood on a narrow strip of land at right angles to the road with the master's house and garden on what is now High Cross Road. On taking up his post as the new master George Nelson Golby wrote, 'The school house is too small; the school itself has very poor accommodation for one of its classes: it consists of one room only which has to serve for instruction and as a refectory for the boys who bring lunch; the sanitary arrangements too are very bad.' Tuition charges were £1 10s annually with 1s 6d charged for the use of books and 6d for the fire.

In 1865 a 'sewing and reading school' was organised, supported by subscriptions from Robert Dunderdale who gave 2 guineas, John Dauntsey, Miss Wilson, Mr Kemp, Mr Rawcliffe and Richard Singleton who each gave £10 and nine and sixpence collected in the alms boxes in the church vestry and the chancel of St Chad's. Old silver coins were sold for 4s 6d and the Revd and Mrs Clark gave 2 guineas. In 1866 the Revd Clark gave a benefit lecture and admission charges raised 17s. With this support from the community it was decided to hire Miss Porter who was paid £3 10s quarterly, to buy twelve copies of Davy's *History of England* from the SPCK and a set of reading books for 8s. But the following year the collection boxes in church raised only 11½d and the vicar gave 6s 5d to prevent the school going into the red. In 1868 Miss Hodge took over as teacher and by 1870 the school budget was balancing at £15 15s 6d per year but the financial burden was being carried by two men – John Daunstey and Robert Dunderdale. In 1874 they decided to close the school.

Admission Number.	Date of Admission. D. M. Y.	NAME (Christian and Surname).	Date of Birth. D. M. Y.		Name and Address of Parent or Guardian.
			18	yrs.	
1	4 1 75	Kate Greenall	11 June 61	14	Richard Greenall
2	" " "	Ellen Jane Atkinson	15 Feb. 63	12	Thomas Atkinson
3	" " "	Emma Jane Riding	3 April 63	12	William Riding
4	" " "	Jane Myerscough	29 May 63	12	John Myerscough
5	" " "	Isabella Roskell	25 Feb. 64	11	John Roskell
6	" " "	Sally Whiteside	9 Sep. 68	7	William Whiteside
7	" " "	Mary Myerscough	24 Aug. 67	8	John Myerscough
8	" " "	Amy Wilson	10 Sep. 64	10	William Wilson
9	" " "	Isabella Atkinson	4 Jan. 65	10	Thomas Atkinson
10	" " "	Hannah Cowell	16 Oct. 63	11	Robert Cowell
11	" " "	Elizabeth Atkinson	12 Jan. 67	7	Thomas Atkinson
12	" " "	Agnes Fairclough	1 Feb. 67	7	Henry Fairclough
13	" " "	Emma Porter	7 May 67	7	Thomas Porter
14	" " "	Isabella Ronson	1 Feb. 66	8	George Ronson
15	" " "	Elizabeth El. Hardicre	16 June 68	6	Henry Hardicre
16	" " "	Emma Bailey	7 Aug. 67	7	William Bailey
17	" " "	Mary Lawrenson	1 July 67	7	Thomas Lawrenson
18	" " "	Mary El. Bailey	8 July 68	6	John Bailey
19	" " "	Margaret Wilkinson	6 Sep. 67	7	Mary Ann Wilkinson

The first record of pupils entering the Church of England school in 1875.

CHAPTER 16

Farming in the Fylde

By the end of the eighteenth century nearly all common fields, often called Town Fields, had been enclosed, new farms established and the land managed, fertilised and fenced, with much of the marsh and moss remaining as common waste and common turbary. By the mid-nineteenth century just a few fields in Poulton still had the old name – two large fields, now covered by Rydal Avenue, were known as Higher and Lower Town End Field. By the early nineteenth century much of the land to the east of Moorland Road was part of the estate of Thomas Fitzherbert Brockholes which he had bought up over the previous years. Two main tenants, Richard Singleton and William Threlfall, were farming the land which accounted for almost 30 per cent of the land in Poulton; in fact in the 1840s 5 per cent of the population owned 54 per cent of the land in the township.

Lancashire was the first county where potatoes were grown and by the mid-1800s were being grown on a grand scale in the Fylde with fields of

The town centre in 1965.

beans, oats and wheat lining the roads. Only the occasional stacks of peat standing outside cottages to be used for fires reminded the inhabitants of the bog, marsh and moss which had once covered large tracts of the Fylde. The eighteenth century saw an improvement in agricultural harvests and an improvement in the country's economy. New ideas in crop rotation and stock breeding were beginning to take effect. The tradition in the Fylde of depositing dung only on the meadow land had left the arable land neglected and in a poor state, but major draining projects of the early nineteenth century and the spreading of 'sea slutch' from the Wyre or marl mixed with peat had produced an improvement in the fertility of the soil. Land which would have been let a few years previously for 5s an acre now brought in 35s, or even £2. Because of the relatively sparse population in the area there was plenty of work available for Irish labourers who arrived in large numbers in early April and returned to Ireland at the end of September. They earned 2s a day and provided their own food although they were given a free quart of butter-milk every day. They slept in barns and outhouses on straw with sacks for pillows. This allowed many to save between £10 and £12 of their wages to take back to Ireland. From the 1840s this annual migration of 'industrious, honest, cheerful, easily managed and well conducted' workers from Ireland had become an essential part of the farming system in the Fylde with the men generally returning to the same farms year after year.

However, Dr Walker, Medical Officer of Health for Fylde Rural District, reported in 1876 that there was serious overcrowding in the summer and autumn months in Poulton, Marton and Staining, resulting from the Irishmen who flocked over in large numbers to assist in the harvest. Although in the past they had been allowed to sleep in the barns and other outbuildings of the farmhouses, it was now decided that this must stop because of the danger from fire. In one case the Medical Officer and the Inspector of Nuisances visited a cottage consisting of a kitchen and two long and narrow rooms used for sleeping, with windows 2ft 5in by 1ft 5in and 9in by 1 ft 1in as ventilation. Over the first of these rooms was a loft, approached by a rickety staircase. In the kitchen were sleeping the occupier and his wife. In the first bedroom the three sons of the tenant slept, in the second bedroom were six lodgers, whilst in the loft were eight lodgers in three beds, 'sleeping without shifts and with only thin counterpanes as coverings. The heat and stench in this place were something dreadful, and how it was possible to sleep, I was at a loss to comprehend'.

As well as health and safety concerns in Poulton about the annual Irish invasion it was also a matter of concern to local labourers that the lower rates paid were keeping wages down for them. Anticipation that this

Farming was the main occupation of the Fylde.

essential source of labour was coming to an end, especially as wage differences between Ireland and the Fylde diminished, may have been a factor in an increasing tendency to lay down permanent pasture and develop dairy farming in the Fylde during the mid-nineteenth century. Added to this, by the 1890s there were severe falls in wheat prices, a crop for which the Fylde had once been well known, as cheaper imports began to arrive from North America.

In 1882 it was estimated that a 100-acre farm – the average size of a farm in the Fylde – would have been able to make about £450 in a year on the sale of wheat, oats, barley, beans and potatoes. Ten years later the income on the same farm had fallen to about £325. As more land was turned over to grass and more farmers moved to dairying, cheese became the one of chief products of the area. The Lancashire long-horned cattle had been well regarded across the country and the best herds were to be found in the Fylde, but by 1850 they had almost disappeared, to be replaced by the milk-producing shorthorns. But the change in farming had come about without provision of suitable accommodation for butter and cheese production or the larger, well ventilated buildings necessary for healthy stock. As a result tuberculosis was rife in the district and a perceived danger to humans of consumption was noted by Poulton's medical officer, Dr John Winn.

Only a few women were employed on farms in the Fylde, usually helping with the harvesting and haymaking. But in Poulton and across much of the Fylde, children were expected to work on farms. In the mid-1860s of the eighty boys attending Poulton Free School the average attendance was no more than forty, and half of the boys were away for periods of five or six months. Most of them left school at eleven. Boys aged between nine and thirteen were employed on farms between May and September and were considered competent to drive a team of horses at twelve. If they were young enough they were expected to attend school for the rest of the year. It was estimated that a third of the children in Poulton parish at this time did not attend school at all. In Fleetwood the children stayed away from school to go cockling, an activity which they started at about eight years old.

Agricultural labourers earned about 12s a week all round the year, out of which they had to pay rent for a cottage, although most farmers had employees, often known as 'farm servants', lodging with them. This latter group fared well; Richard Cookson who farmed at Layton Hawes supplied his six farm servants with five meals a day and fresh meat twice a day and milk or butter-milk – no beer. The cottages Cookson provided for his labourers had slated roofs and three bedrooms – an improvement of the two-room mud and cobble cottages with thatched roofs which they replaced. Gardens were cultivated for food by the families so there was no need for separate allotments. Cookson considered the improvement in living conditions had led to a decrease in the number of illegitimate children being born and a general improvement in the morality in Great Marton. As a Poor Law Guardian he recalled once seeing thirty-eight bastardy cases in one day at the Petty Sessions.

CHAPTER 17

Pubs, Clubs and Houses

During the nineteenth century attorneys and surgeons, bakers and flour dealers, boot and shoemakers, braziers and tin-plate workers, butchers and coopers, corn millers and corn merchants, grocers, ironmongers, drapers and painters, plumbers and glaziers, saddlers and straw hatmakers, tailors and wheelwrights provided almost every service the inhabitants from the neighbouring townships could need within a short travelling distance. There were three annual market days for cattle, cloth and household goods, there was a daily horse post to and from Preston and a foot post to Blackpool daily in the 'bathing season' and on Monday, Wednesday and Saturday in the winter. Three carriers took goods and parcels to Lancaster, Liverpool and Preston weekly, returning the following day.

Poulton was the centre of a major agricultural area and catered well for the pleasures of the working population. A cluster of public houses and several beer sellers meant that the men of the town looking for a convivial evening were well catered for. The public houses included the Kings Arms in the Market Place, the Black Bull and Sportsman's Arms in Bull Street, the Ship on the corner of the Breck and Vicarage Road, a short distance from the Golden Ball, the Plough and the Bay Horse in Church Street, the Thatched House at the church gate. Away from the town centre was the Railway and Station hotel built a year before the railway line was completed in 1840. By the 1930s this had ceased to be a hotel and had been turned into flats. On the opposite corner of Station Road, once known as Back Lane, the Royal Oak Hotel was built later in

Church Street with the Bay Horse on the left, the Plough on the far left and the Golden Ball in the distance.

The Market Place, c. 1900. The King's Arms at the far end of the property on the left was demolished in the 1920s.

the 1840s and housed the Inland Revenue office. The site had originally been occupied by a dye works. At Skippool was the Brockhole Arms, apparently known in the 1820s as the Saracen's Head. The landlords of the Bull, the Golden Ball, the Royal Oak and the Railway took in paying guests and regarded their properties as hotels, while the rest were taverns and public houses. The outbuildings of the old Kings Arms in the Market Place were turned into a sort of general assembly room for the town, with various kinds of shows, from marionettes to bloodcurdling plays, dances, market hall and occasional sales being held there. In the 1920s it became home of the Comrades of the Great War Association, but the buildings were destroyed by fire in 1940. The Ship Inn has had a mixed career; the galleon design depicting its name can still be seen in the brickwork. It was remembered as hosting hard drinking, rowdy and sometimes 'brutal drinkers' – seamen from Fleetwood, navvies on construction work and harvesters from Ireland, as well as the regular locals among the farmers and tradesmen. It was popular with the men who worked the trotting track at Skippool and the touts and bookies – trotting ponies were often stabled at the Ship – as well as promoters and supporters of whippet racing, and pigeon fanciers. After a few years serving as the local Working Men's Club, in December 1927 a public meeting was held to discuss a proposal to take it over as the Conservative Club and it opened its doors as such on 4 February 1928, closing in 2001. The Black Bull had a large figure of a bull complete with horns standing above the doorway until rebuilding work took place in the 1950s. It was one of Poulton's coaching inns and the coaches drawn by two, three or sometimes four horses would pass up Breck Road and stop at the Black Bull Hotel in the Market Place

Bull Street in the late 1960s. The Black Bull pub is on the far right and the Sportsman's Arms in the block on the left.

on their way to Blackpool. In 1896 the sign of the old Bull, which had been stored away for some time, was back in its original position on the front wall of the hotel but when the pub was rebuilt 1955 the Bull sign was seen no more.

The Plough faced St Chad's on Church Street and in 1792 was described as a one-bay dwelling house built of brick and covered with thatch with a brewhouse, swine-cotes, gardens and a stable. At the south end was a right of way which allowed for horses to pass and from the stable and for thatching to be done. The passageway is still there but now it leads to a car park. The Plough disappeared in the rebuilding of the west side of Church Street in the early 1900s just as a new pub, The Queens, was being licensed in the Green. The Sportsman Arms on Bull Street became the Merry England, a well known cake shop and café. The Bay Horse opposite St Chad's became the offices of Poulton Urban District Council. When reorganisation of local government saw the introduction of Wyre Borough Council with new offices at the bottom of the Breck the building once again became a pub – now known as The Old Town Hall.

The Golden Ball was another of Poulton's coaching inns. On 4 June 1811 a 'Coffee Room' was set up in the pub with a committee of five local men. It soon began to serve as the town's reading room and paid for itself by subscriptions and the sale of newspapers which in the early days included the *Evening Mail*, the *Preston Chronicle* and the *Liverpool*

An early picture of the Golden Ball.

The Auction Mart in around 1900 looking towards the entrance to the Golden Ball.

Mercury. By the mid-nineteenth century more newspapers and periodicals were available for those whose reading skills were above average, including some which are still familiar today. *The Standard, The Globe, The Liverpool Times, The Liverpool Mercury* and *The Manchester Guardian* provided Poulton with national and international news. *The Farmers' Journal, The New Monthly Magazine, The Quarterly Review, The Edinburgh Review, The Penny Magazine* and *Bell's Messenger* catered for all tastes and interests. The Golden Ball also became the venue for the court for petty sessions. The first county court was held in April 1847 and it was not until the 1880s that it was transferred to Blackpool so Blackpool people not only did their shopping in Poulton but their legal business also.

In 1898 several major building projects were started: in September the old police station in the Market Place was demolished, its replacement designed by William Cardwell of Blackpool. In October of that year the foundation stone of the Masonic Hall was laid but the most important undertaking was the new auction mart. Taking in all the land at the back of the Golden Ball it cost £800 to build and was the very latest in design with a weighbridge, showring and auctioneer's rostrum and accommodation for sixty to seventy cattle and pens for 500 sheep. Its first show and sale showed 'good prices': 'fatstock made up to £18, heifers had brought £15, calves £4 to £6, lambs 32s to 42s.' The depression in farming had not affected the Fylde with its concentration on pasture and the heavy manuring of farmland had resulted in 'immense crops and large haystacks' the previous year. Passing into the auction mart from Ball Street on the right was the 'Irish yard' a large building with double doors, big enough for a cattle wagon to reverse in to the building and unload bulls in safety. Next to the Irish yard was the bullring, a shippon with about forty stalls, each with a manger and a slaughter-house. On the left were offices, a circular calf ring and sheep pens, loose boxes for horses and covered pens, and at the far end the midden – a boon to all the allotment holders and gardeners in Poulton. Some of the iron rings used to tie up the animals are still in place. Traders in farm tools, saws, knives, leggings and corduroy trousers visited the auctions. Cattle would be driven up the Breck to the auction mart and shopkeepers nearby would make a barrier with their bikes across the road to drive the animals through the entrance. When the sale was a few days away they would be driven to fields behind Chatsworth House – close to the present day Chester Avenue. Several times during the year flocks of geese from Ireland were driven from the station to the auction mart field for farmers to fatten up for Christmas. At Christmas the auction would deal with over 9,000 birds. In the 1920s there would be as many as eight sales a week and 6,000 head of stock would be handled in one day.

At the back of the tithe barn were workshops and, further out, greenhouses and the fields of the market gardeners who grew salad crops in the summer and chrysanthemums in the winter. During the Second World War the fields were commandeered to grow vegetables but cereal crops were to prove more successful – the chrysanths had to be grown elsewhere.

The Spread Eagle stood in Queens Square and is easily recognisable today as a three-storey, double-fronted building with large double gates to one side through which the horses would have passed to the stables at the back. The original cobbles can still be seen. At ground floor level were shops, one of which was a grocer's run by Robert Parkinson, a flour dealer and baker. His initials R.A.P. were set in tiles in the doorway and into a decorative plaque above the first floor windows. Robert Parkinson's eldest daughter Agnes had married William Tomlinson, who ran the corn mill behind the shops in Queens Square accessed through the gateway of the old Spread Eagle inn. The property, which incorporated a jam factory, a café and a grocer's, ran from Queens Square through to Chapel Street Court where a coffee shop now commemorates the corn mill which once stood there. The Parkinson family lived above the grocers' shop and above the café was a lecture room that was hired out for public functions. A frieze illustrating the four seasons is set into the wall above the old entrance to the mill. Agnes and William Tomlinson had two sons whose names are remembered down the years: Robert Parkinson Tomlinson, known as 'Parky-Tomlinson' and John Maynard Tomlinson, a well known amateur photographer in the Fylde. In 1875 when the Congregational church was undergoing repair, services were held in the rooms of Robert Parkinson Tomlinson, a member of the church. Hugh Parkinson, brother of Agnes, was registrar of births, marriages and deaths at the turn of the twentieth century and had his office in the back rooms.

The Thatched House, standing close to one of the church gates, is a reminder of the long journey by foot which inhabitants of the great parish of Poulton had to undertake each Sunday. In need of refreshment, they would have made use of the pub's hospitality. Records show that there was a pub known as the Green Man in Breck Street in the early nineteenth century run by the Hardman family. From later records it would seem likely that this property changed its name to the Thatched House. The earliest landlord recorded was Thomas Hardman in the 1820s, by the 1840s he had been succeeded by his son George; both he and his sister Jane, a schoolmistress who lived next door to the pub were born in Liverpool. George and Mary Hardman were in turn succeeded by their son Thomas and his wife. Margaret, Thomas's second wife was the daughter of Henry Curwen who in the early nineteenth century ran a ferry boat across the Wyre from the Shard Inn to the south bank of the river. The original Thatched House stood sideways on to the churchyard. It was demolished in 1910 as part of the planned removal of old properties that backed on to the churchyard and was replaced by the mock Tudor building of today.

Horse-drawn wagonettes carried parties around the Fylde countryside, stopping for refreshments at the small towns. Poulton with its pubs was a great attraction for these groups. One fine Sunday morning in the early 1900s several wagonettes pulled up outside the Thatched House where they were served ham and eggs. Unfortunately they completely blocked

The Breck and the Thatched House in the 1920s. The garden on the far right belonged to a large house called Tower Lodge, which was turned into shops in the 1930s.

The original Thatched House was replaced in 1910. Here both buildings can be seen.

the entrance to St Chad's preventing parishioners getting into church. The vicar was understandably irate and unceremoniously strode into the pub to register a protest.

Sheaf Street became Hardhorn Road just before the Second World War but many people continued to use its old name. It was named after the Wheatsheaf Inn which stood on the southern corner of what is now the Hardhorn Road car park. The inn became a private house in the early 1820s. It had a varied career, serving as the town's first telephone exchange and lastly the home of the Comrades Club. The outside of the building with its Georgian portico remained unchanged until demolition. Inside the small rooms had thick walls, the cellars arched roofs of enormous strength and thickness and at each side the windows had specially constructed doors that folded into little alcoves.

In 1873 Poulton was described as having 'an air of quiet gentility and serene independence about the place, the houses clean and old fashioned, some with an anciently aristocratic look'. Large, white, three-storey, double-fronted Georgian family houses lined the main streets; owned by attorneys and solicitors, they contrasted sharply with the rough workshops and sheds, small shops and two-storey cobble cottages which stood side by side with them on Ball Street and Tithebarn Street, Sheaf Street, Bull Street and the Market Place. Property at the top of the Breck illustrated this mix with the home of the Thornber family on the west side, now with shop fronts on the ground floor, and on the east side a row of small thatched cottages and workshops including a joiner, a slater and a blacksmith's, the last building before the station. The present red brick shop fronts date from the early 1900s. Except for two or three old family houses there were no buildings further down the Breck than the present railway station in the 1840s. By the 1880s this had become the desirable part of the town and there was land available for building. The large family houses built on Breck Road were bought by a mixture of local people and Lancashire industrialists. Thomas Hanesworth was a manufacturing chemist from Great Lever with his wife, five children and a governess; John Wynn, a GP from Ireland; Charles Axon, a land and buildings inspector from Heaton Norris; Richard Lambert, minister of the Independent chapels in Poulton and Hambleton came from Bispham; George Catterall, a Baptist minister from St Michaels, and Henry Copeland from Woodplumpton, a veterinary surgeon. John McKane Cryer from Bolton was the head of a large iron foundry who moved to Poulton with his wife and daughters. When John McKane Cryer died in 1910 the four sisters, Bertha, Edith, Ethel and Anne, opened a school in the family house, known as 'Miss Cryer's', which ran until 1947.

The large family houses being built on the Breck in the 1880s attracted local people too and Robert Dunderdale made another move from his house in Queens Square to a new one on the Breck, named Clifton House. As Breck Road became lined with new property so streets were developed running off the main road into the fields. In 1879 plans and agreements were drawn up to build a row of houses with a back street and two roads on a four-acre field to the north of Breck Road known as Cottam Carr Field, owned by the descendants of William Elletson. Those roads were to become Elletson Street and Derby Road. By 1840 William Elletson of Parrox Hall owned virtually all the property on the south side of Queens Square including the fields behind it, almost down to the school building on Wheatsheaf Street, an area of land now the site of Princess Avenue, and Cottam Carr Field.

Charabanc trips were very popular, first horse-drawn as here in the early years of the twentieth century, and later motorised versions, up to the 1930s.

The Breck was not typical; a more socially mixed group lived in Sheaf Street: three farmers and a farm labourer, a property owner, a blacksmith, a cattle dealer, three annuitants living on private income, a railway platelayer, the registrar, two joiners and a mill owner from Liverpool. Poulton also catered for numbers of travellers and hawkers who came to the town and stayed in lodging houses in Church Street, and Potts Alley – also known as Potts Entry or Potts Lane. This latter became renowned as 'a dangerous place for young ladies', warned to keep away by their fathers. The Market Place also had a mix of houses, shops and works. On the east side stood an imposing double-fronted, three-storey house which had once been the home of the Walmsleys. In the mid-nineteenth century it became the police station and in 1898 it was demolished to be replaced by the Masonic Hall. The present police station stands next to it. The site of the National Westminster Bank was once the town house of Alexander Rigby.

Entertainment in Poulton was plentiful and included lectures with

Lockwood Avenue one of the popular residential roads developed in the late 1880s.

Sheaf Street still has a number of older properties surviving today.

Carleton tithe map of 1839 showing the Weld Arms, now the Castle Gardens, at Four Lane Ends.

lantern slides, tea-parties, hotpot suppers and garden parties, musical and dramatic entertainments, plays, concerts and recitals. Fundraising for churches, schools, charities and good causes was a constant issue and generated a programme of bazaars, sales of work and jumble sales. Occasionally the vicarage gardens were thrown open, with games and music provided and most national celebrations entailed festivities with a procession, a meal for the elderly and games for the children in a local field or garden. The Castle Gardens at Four Lane Ends, Carleton, was a pleasant inn and park area with a menagerie and entertainments. There is a record of somewhere called The Hole i' the Wall at Carleton, possibly the forerunner of the present pub, which appears to have been built in 1831. In that year John Kirkham, who rented the mill at Carleton for £58 per annum, was paid £15 9s 6d for carting materials to 'the new public house in Carleton'. At the time much of the land in Carleton belonged to Joseph Weld and the new pub reflected this, being known as the Weld Arms. Robert Carter, a Poulton mineral water manufacturer, was landlord until the late 1880s when the pub was renamed the Castle Gardens.

By 1912 Poulton Chrysanthemum and Horticultural Society was flourishing. Poulton Brass Band, founded in September 1875, was often to be heard playing at galas, garden parties and civic occasions. Cricket had been popular since the early nineteenth century. A notebook records that in 1838 a bet was placed on a match to be played at Kirkham between the cricket clubs of Poulton and Kirkham: 'George Whitton bets George Armstrong and William Dagger each one bottle of wine that the Poulton Cricket Club beats the Kirkham Cricket Club in a match to be played on the 28th instant on the Kirkham cricket ground. Witnessed by Robert Hornby Porter.' There is an addition: 'If John Williamson should happen to join the Poulton

Cycling became very popular in the late nineteenth century with cycling clubs formed in Blackpool, Cleveleys and Fleetwood, riding as far as the Trough of Bowland.

Carleton School is one of the oldest schools in the Fylde, founded as a result of the provision of Elizabeth Wilson, who died in 1680.

Gentlemen in the above match the above wagers shall be declared void'! Football teams were formed and Poulton Amateurs, Poulton Institute and various church teams competed in local leagues. Fishing went on in the many ponds and marl pits, in the River Wyre and Fleetwood Docks, and Poulton Angling Society was formed. Pigeon-racing and pigeon-shooting prospered, Poulton Tennis Club was successful and golf was played at Poulton Links. Cycling was flourishing across the country and there were local clubs at Cleveleys, Fleetwood and Blackpool. The sport had begun in the 1870s and bicycles became cheaper. In Poulton the 'Cyclists' Rest', a temperance inn on the Market Square was very popular between 1890 and 1910. Many people had bicycles and enjoyed rides to the Trough of Bowland. The Institute was a Working Men's Club, which offered leisure time with friends and was organised on non-political and non-sectarian

The Castle Gardens had various entertainments in the late nineteenth century.

An entrance to the churchyard from the Market Place flanked by some of the oldest property in Poulton.

A seventeenth-century road map showing the route from Poulton to Lancaster, showing the bullring in the Market place and the home of Mr Pattison – Breck House.

lines. Open to all comers, the subscription was 5s per annum. Classes for adults were also put on at the Institute, but judging by the constant reminders issued to the public in the early years, support for these classes was perhaps disappointing.

Horse drawn wagonettes took groups all over the Fylde and in 1875 the first St Chad's Sunday school day trip to Lytham took place and so many went it was said the town was emptied. Each year around sixteen charabancs went on the annual outing to Lytham carrying nearly 400 people. The party stopped at Little Marton to rest the horses. Lunch at the Assembly Rooms in Lytham, then a picture show, followed by tea and a walk round the shops and they were welcomed back into Poulton Market Place by cheering crowds and the ringing of the church bells.

Benjamin Corless Sykes was a solicitor who in 1886 decided to speculate and bought Eryngo Lodge which he opened as the highly successful Cleveleys Hydro. In 1895 Sykes built a grand house in Poulton, that he named The Manor, on land just off Moorland Road at a cost of over £12,000 – a huge sum at the time. In the early 1900s he opened it to the public as an exhibition place for art and curios, offering afternoon teas and organising trips from Cleveleys and Blackpool. An advertisement in *The Blackpool, Lytham & Fleetwood Gazette* reads: 'To Blackpool visitors – New drive to the magnificent country mansion, The Manor, Poulton-le-Fylde. Ornamental gardens, and extensive collection of pictures and art treasures. Admission 6d, Children 3d. Teas and other refreshments, Tuesdays and Thursday 1s. (Tea included). Closed on Sundays.' The Manor was also within walking distance of Poulton station. The building later became a private house, a vegetarian guest house, the training school for Rediffusion and finally a nursing home.

For most of the nineteenth century a large residence called Breck House, standing at the bottom of the Breck, was owned by the Catterall family, James Sykes taking up residence there in the early 1870s. The house, is recorded by name on a rare road map showing the route from Poulton to Lancaster which dates from 1684. In 1732 the churchwardens of Poulton together with the Overseers of the Poor of Poulton, Hardhorn, Thornton, Claughton, Garstang, Goosnargh, Pilling and Marton drew up an agreement for 'the lodging, maintaining and employing' of poor people from their parishes to come to a shared workhouse in Poulton. The record refers to a house in Poulton called 'Breckhouse' which was contracted from Mrs Hayhurst, widow of William Hayhurst, for a period of fifty years with each of the contributing parishes paying a share of the costs. It is not clear now when this building was altered or perhaps rebuilt but its appearance at its recent demolition (1998) was apparently early twentieth century. It was most recently used, with several extensions added, as the Mary Macarthy convalescent home and it is possible that earlier building structures were hidden within the shell of the later building.

CHAPTER 18

The Twentieth Century

In 1900 the Parish Council became Poulton Urban District Council, after an election in which only 433 out of the population of 1,000 were eligible to vote. A clerk to the council was engaged at £30 per annum and a surveyor and sanitary inspector at £80. At its first meeting held in the Technical Institute, William Hodgson was elected chairman having polled by far the largest number of votes. The Hodgson family lived at The Sycamores on Blackpool Old Road opposite the library.

William Hodgson was the son of Braithwaite Bond, one-time Poulton auctioneer, and his wife Margaret Hodgson. Margaret's father William and his brother John had done well from a successful tanning business in Poulton and both had retired early on the proceeds. The two men's wives, who were the sisters Ellen and Jane Lewtas, had both died young and William was the only heir. The elder William came to an arrangement with his grandson: if he would take his mother's maiden name as his own and thereby continue the family line he would inherit his grandfather's property. This duly happened. William Hodgson served as a churchwarden at St Chad's for many years. He became chairman of Lancashire County Council and was knighted in 1935. He died on 3 March 1945.

St Chad's churchyard underwent a redesign and a long row of poplars was planted on the south side. Beds were cut and planted; elms, sycamores and beeches which had been planted in the churchyard in 1848 were by 1902 causing havoc with the drains and so were removed and new drains were laid on the north side. St Chad's is well known for its snowdrops, daffodils and crocuses in the spring but it is difficult to put a date on when this planting began. William Lawrenson, captain of the bellringers for thirty years and verger until he retired in 1952, is remembered as having done much to tend annual displays of spring flowers in the churchyard and the process of replanting continues today.

The Lancashire Parish Register Society was founded in 1898 with the purpose of making printed copies of old parish registers in the county. The society, along with many others set up in counties across England, was determined to rescue those old registers still remaining and print those still readable and in 1903 Mr W.E. Robertson began the work on volume one, covering the period from 1591 to 1677. Sadly volume two never materialised.

Over a period of about ten years, from the late 1890s, negotiations had

William Hodgson.

William Lawrenson sweeping up leaves in the churchyard.

Another of the four entrances to the churchyard showing some of the old buildings that were destined to be demolished in 1910.

been going on to arrange compensation for those who owned properties abutting the churchyard in Church Street and Ball Street. Eventually, in 1910, a series of shops, workshops, stables and shippons in these streets were demolished and Ball Street was widened.

An imposing building once stood facing the Market Place on the corner with Church Street, forming a right angle with a pair of lodging houses. A significant slope between the frontage on the Market Place and that in Church Street meant the lodging house had a cellar at ground level and the front door had to be reached by a double set of steps by which it acquired the name 'Twenty Steps'. This house provided a temporary home for pedlars, hawkers and 'harvestmen' along with similar lodging houses in Potts Alley. When the buildings in Ball Street were demolished the foundation of the present churchyard wall built in 1911 had to be laid on old graves. Tradition says a date was chiselled on the back of the first stone near the Thatched House and a bottle was buried under it containing some newspapers and coins. The County Bank building, once the Cyclists Rest, was left standing and faced with stone to match the stone of the wall. In the autumn of 1938 the County Council bought the bank with the aim of pulling it down and adding the land to the Market Place and the job was completed the following summer. It is thought that some oak panelling from the old building went to decorate a property at Scorton and some of the masonry became the corner stone of a café at Gisburn in Yorkshire.

In the early years of the twentieth century, just as in most of the nineteenth, children in Poulton were often absent from school through family workload, illness and bad weather. It was not unusual for schools to be closed for periods of up to six weeks by an outbreak of measles. Scarlet fever, chicken pox, mumps, measles and whooping cough and influenza were prevalent and school closures were usually followed by a visit from the sanitary department to fumigate the buildings. Cramped conditions contributed to the problems – in 1928 an inspector reported that in one Poulton school there were 305 children in four rooms: 'At the visit there were 110 infants being taught in one room with no free space for movement.' One way round the problem was to 'promote' children to the next class throughout the year so the composition of each class was constantly changing. Year after year school log books record epidemics of all the childhood diseases to the extent that the attendance in Poulton schools often fell to below 50 per cent and schools expected to close for several weeks each year.

Land belonging to Normoss Farm was purchased by the Manchester and Salford Society for the Reformation of Juvenile Offenders in 1905 and as Fylde Farm School and latterly as Fylde School it continued to serve youngsters with problems who came from a wide area. At the annual prize distribution on Thursday 30 December 1905 Mr and Mrs Potter entertained a large number of visitors including Mr Harold Lee JP, Chairman of the Governors, and Mr J. Lewis Paton, MA, High Master of Manchester Grammar School, who addressed the school and gave away the prizes. A special conduct prize, a silver watch, was awarded to the best behaved boy in the school. Three years later 176 old boys of the school were fighting in France.

The world was soon to change. Perhaps Robert Parkinson Tomlinson JP, chairman of Poulton Urban District Council, had foresight of this when in 1910 he requested a Civic and Military Service be held at St Chad's, with a military parade to the church lead by Poulton Prize Band. On 24 February 1914 a Sgt Beckenham took part in an 'entertainment' consisting of songs, solos and dances, and recited 'The Charge of the Light Brigade' and talked about his experiences in the trenches during the Crimean War – a foretaste of the war to come. By August 1915 a number of men and women had already enlisted when a recruiting meeting was held in the Market Place in September. It resulted in over forty volunteers leaving Poulton station on 5 October each with a very hearty send-off and a present donated by the social club. By November the first casualties and internments among local men and women were being recorded. In Poulton working parties were set up to produce garments for the forces: 185 flannel shirts, 202 body belts, 316 pairs of socks, 53 night shirts, 24 bed jackets, 4 dressing gowns, 15 sets of pyjamas, 94 woollen scarves, 45 helmets, 43 pairs of mittens and 34 pillows were among the items sent off in 1915. Others volunteered for the Territorials and went into training in Lancaster. An ambulance class was begun through which thirty young men and women were trained and a branch of St John Ambulance was formed ready for duty. Several people made use of their training by

Church Street, in the 1900s. The tree in the centre is still there today.

Tithebarn Street with the tithe barn on the right and some fine residential properties on the left, all demolished in recent years.

assisting the nurses at Blackpool Victoria Hospital. The annual Sunday school trip to Lytham was cancelled in part due to shortages brought on by the war of horses, wagons, men and food. Much effort went in to raising money for various aspects of the war effort – the Prince of Wales' Fund, the Belgian Soldiers' Fund, the Belgian Refugee Fund and the Belgian Famine Fund. Shortage of labour and difficulties in getting goods hampered local shopkeepers who requested that orders should be placed early in the day and small parcels carried whenever convenient.

Many of the features of Poulton which are so familiar to present-day inhabitants appeared at this time. In June 1916 William Hughes of Warbreck Drive and Mrs Sarah Brown of Buchanan Street, Blackpool, built the Rialto cinema in Vicarage Road. Unfortunately the venture failed and they were declared bankrupt the following year. In 1922 a memorial commemorating the dead of the war was placed in St Chad's and a new war memorial erected in Queens Square. Work began on St Chad's church hall in 1925. In 1926 a Memorial Park was opened marking the life of nine-year-old Jean Stansfield, the new Diocese of Blackburn was created, the new road from Poulton to Singleton was opened and the first Child Welfare Centre was opened in the new Church Hall by Lancashire County Council.

A visit by the Prince Of Wales to Poulton in June 1927 saw the streets decorated in welcome. Poulton's first purpose built secondary school was opened in 1932 named after Sir William Hodgson. At its opening pupils over eleven years transferred to it from Poulton, Carleton, Staining, Singleton and Hambleton. Sheaf Street Church of England School became a school for infants and juniors only.

In the mid-1930s started a period of demolition and rebuilding in the

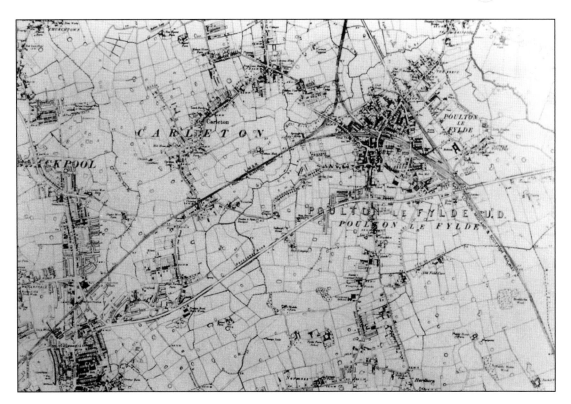

A map of 1930 showing Poulton and Carleton.

town centre which continued right up to the late 1960s and saw the destruction of several Georgian properties replaced by purpose-built shops. 'Tower Lodge', an imposing Victorian property which stood close to the station entrance on the Breck, a large, three-storey property on the corner of Ball Street and Church Street and the last property backing into the churchyard, all went in the late 1930s. Others were saved from demolition but had their ground floor spaces converted into shops. Poulton was changing and people bemoaned the changes. The old house of Kirkham's on the Breck now had chromium-plated shops of the ultra modern style in great contrast to the rest of the shops in the immediate vicinity. The corner of Sheaf Street and Queens Square was bought by the council for road widening and the old county court was rebuilt as the town library which had up to then been housed in the town hall.

In December 1936 fire struck the Market Place when the printers' shop, run for three generations by the Smith family, was seriously damaged and Tom Smith himself died. His grandfather had been responsible for printing the first history of the area, *Thornber's History of Blackpool and its Neighbourhood*, and his great-grandfather had been headmaster of the Free School from 1825 to 1831.

On several occasions in the 1930s plans were discussed to amalgamate Poulton with Blackpool, but local feeling was against it and on each

occasion it was rejected. In 1946 local authorities and the County Council were again discussing boundaries and Poulton was presented with a choice – to join with Thornton Cleveleys UDC or amalgamate with Blackpool County Council. A plan was drawn up which envisaged the population growing to 25,000 by 1971. Three secondary schools were to be built on new roads to the north of Moorland Road behind Little Poulton Lane, a community centre on High Cross Road, swimming baths on land behind Queen's Square and a business centre in the Market Place. After much discussion and some close votes over a period of twelve months, the minutes of Poulton UDC record that 'conversations with Blackpool Corporation on the matter of district boundaries were for the purposes only of information and guidance and in no way commit this council'. After that the whole question died a natural death.

In June 1938 the town's first public bowling green was opened in the Jean Stansfield Memorial Park, by an official party including Robert Parkinson, one of the earliest members of the local council. The Stansfields had bought some of the church glebe land bordered by Station Road and Vicarage Road. Mr Stansfield had died in 1932 so it had required Mrs Stansfield, of Blackpool Old Road, to allow alterations to the deeds relating to the park to permit the laying of the green on the south side of Memorial Park, close to St Chad's football ground. A pavilion built of rustic brick was surrounded by shrubs given by Messrs B. Windsor and Sons. Inside was a greenkeeper's table, and a series of bowls shelves and space for lockers, all neatly indexed.

The company 'Windsor Woollies' was well-known at this time and had begun in Colne in 1905 with Benjamin and Elizabeth Windsor where they were the caretakers of Alkincoates Hall. Elizabeth, an excellent needlewoman, made clothes for their two sons William and Albert on a hand-knitting machine and a shop soon opened in the front room of their terraced house in Brown Street, Colne, selling baby wear and shawls. During the First World War they made khaki pullovers for the troops. After several moves to larger premises in Colne the business moved to Buchanan Street in Blackpool in 1923 and five years later a new factory opened in Station Road, Poulton. In the 1960s another branch opened in Garstang and later the Poulton factory closed.

In September 1939 with a war threatening the County Council appropriated the Church Hall to be used as a first aid post. The following year Poulton itself began to experience something of the war. On 30 August a German plane dropped three bombs on North Shore Golf Links and on 2 September the siren placed on St Chad's church tower was sounded for the first time at 10.45 p.m. Planes were heard

The old vicarage was demolished in the 1950s.

passing over but no bombs were dropped. In September eight bombs dropped near Kirkham. On 19 October three bombs were dropped in a field on the Brockholes at the end of Compley Avenue, two exploded but no damage was done and no-one was hurt. Four days later the third bomb finally exploded at 10.30 p.m. but again there was no damage. Other bombs dropped near Baines School, the loud bang frightening a little girl who had been reading in bed by the light of a candle and 'thought the planes must have been able to see it'.

Winter 1941 saw snow so deep that children walked along the tops of hedges and many from outlying areas could not get to school for some weeks. In response to the war and clothes rationing in 1942 the Archbishops of Canterbury and York decided that women could attend church without wearing hats. The same year saw some of the iron railings in St Chad's churchyard removed for the war effort, but the gates and rails round individual graves were saved. Children were issued with gas masks and were expected to take them to school each day or they would be sent home to get them. Many did forget them and so had more time out of lessons. 600 children were evacuated to the Poulton area and it was planned to accommodate 200 from Salford in the school on Sheaf Street with local children attending in the morning and the visitors in the afternoon. At Christmas that year many evacuees returned home and a number did not return. By January 1940 the number was under 100 and in September arrangements were made for the evacuees to have their schooling in the Congregational Sunday school in Tithebarn Street so the children of Sheaf Street School went back to normal lessons.

After the war new house building projects began in Poulton. In 1949

Kings Close, Queens Close and Princess Avenue were built on farmland which had been compulsorily purchased. A regular visitor to the farm there had been a local artist and signwriter Alphonso Wing who in return for breakfasts, apple pie and cheese, painted a picture of the farmhouse. In 1923 he hand-tinted the print of the Market Place which had been published by Arkwright and Lawrenson in 1898.

In 1951 the old vicarage and grounds were sold to the Poulton Council. The new one was to be built higher up the road and a £10,000 scheme for converting the old vicarage into a town hall was discussed. While the future of the old vicarage was being decided, preparations were being made to open the gardens to the public and a new park was formed in the grounds.

Probably most towns and villages in the country can look back to the 1950s and '60s with regret for what was lost. It was a period of demolition and rebuilding and sadly some of the buildings lost would today have been cherished and preserved. In Poulton it was the tithe barn. The system of tithes began in the seventh century and Poulton's tithe barn occupied a site very close to St Chad's church fronting on to one of the six main roads leading off the Market Place. The siting of the tithe barn so close to the church suggests it was ancient although no date was ever attributed to it. During the bathing season visitors would come to Poulton from Blackpool and would be entertained by performances in the barn which by 1822 was in use as a theatre, at a time before there were any in Blackpool. At other times of the year the tithe barn was used for threshing. In 1951 the Council discussed the possibility of preserving the tithe barn as a museum, but nothing was done and in June 1968 the local newspaper reported a move by the Poulton Round Table to save the tithe barn from the bulldozers

The tithe barn in use by Parkinson Tomlinson, the millers.

following a talk by the county archaeologist to the group. Plans were made to save the barn by public subscription with help from the County Council and the Ministry of Works. The effort was unsuccessful and the tithe barn was demolished.

In 1953 Queen Elizabeth was crowned and the nation watched the coronation ceremony for the first time on television; in Poulton it was possible to watch it at the Rialto cinema or in the church hall, free of charge. Two years later a town map laying out proposals for the next twenty years was published. It was suggested that Poulton's population might reach 27,000 but by 1955 this figure had been drastically reduced to 15,000 under the new plan. The following year Poulton's new county primary school, with one class of thirty children aged five, opened in temporary accommodation in the Festival Hall on Blackpool Old Road pending the arrival of the new building on Carr Head Lane.

The rate of growth in house building in Poulton in the 1950s was very rapid and in 1955 there was no Poulton Gala because land was no longer available as a Gala field. Instead there was a children's treat with film show at the Rialto a meal and sports in the evening on Wednesday 27 July during the school holidays. Poulton Gala had started as a club day in 1795 when the event was organised by the joint effort of two friendly societies, the Royal Union, whose meeting place was the Bull Hotel, and the Good Samaritans who met at the Golden Ball. They met each year on the first Wednesday after 24 June then proceeded to the vicarage and along with the vicar, clergy and church officers walked to the church where prayers were said and a short address given by the vicar. In 1897 the name was changed and club day became known as Poulton Children's Festival when for the first time the children took an active part in it and paraded in character costume in a procession. With only two breaks during the two wars it has carried on continuously to the present day.

1955 saw another major re-ordering of St Chad's and, in an effort to simplify the interior, it was redesigned incorporating a centre aisle and a new Jacobean-style pulpit was designed to incorporate five ancient panels which were found in the church in 1877 when the previous pulpit was removed.

In recent years new developments in the town have included a swimming pool, a golf course, pedestrianisation of the Market Place, new sheltered accommodation and a good deal of new housing.

The history of Poulton is that of a small market town which for centuries served many isolated hamlets and farmsteads as a centre for exchange and bartering, buying and selling, socialising and entertainment and as a centre for churchgoing, lawgiving and support.

Poulton remained untouched by the development of industries which consumed much of Lancashire during the nineteenth century and has emerged in the twenty-first century as a flourishing community of over 20,000 people. There is, as always, a balance to be struck between preserving the unique characteristics of the town and the commercial and residential development necessary for its continued prosperity.

Poulton developed rapidly in the 1960s.

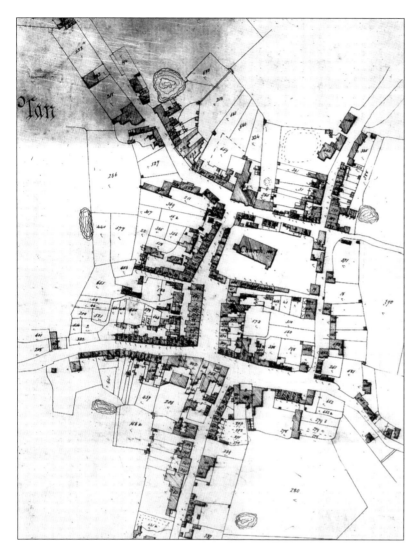

The tour takes visitors round the town centre, beginning outside the parish church.

Walking Tour

The Market Place in 2000.

Exactly one hundred years separates these photographs of the Market Place. In the distance on the left can be seen a row of thatched cottages which included the Plough Inn. The Cyclists' Rest was very popular at the time and stood on the site of the original Moot Hall of medieval times. The building later became a bank and was demolished in 1938.

The same view in 1900.

Stand in the Market Place with your back to St Chad's church.

Fairs and markets have been held in this square for centuries. In medieval times it would have been surrounded by cobble-built cottages, thatched with reeds from the River Wyre with one or two large town houses built by local gentry who came to Poulton in the winter months. The buildings running down the right-hand side are all similar in style because they were built at the same time by public subscription after a disastrous fire of 1732 when the whole of the west side of the Market Place was burned down. The shop at the far end on the right was an ironmonger's for several generations and is well known to local people as Richards'. The shop now the Trustees Savings Bank was a stationers and printers in the early nineteenth century run by Thomas Smith, where William Thornber's *History of Blackpool* was published in 1837. On the left is the police station and Masonic Hall; the latter was built in 1897 on the site of a three-storey, double-fronted town house. The building immediately on the left is one of the oldest buildings in Poulton with one wall actually in the churchyard. The interior has been much altered and modernised. The war memorial was moved to this position in the early 1970s but was originally erected in 1922 in Queens Square.

St Chad's parish church.

Turn right into Church Street.

On a shop front opposite the church is a plaque marking the site of the Plough Inn. Next to it is a passageway where tenants of the Plough had a right of way to the back of the pub enabling them to reach the stable there and thatch the roof. This was one of a dozen pubs catering for farmers and labourers coming into the town on market days from outlying villages. The Old Town Hall pub was originally the Bay Horse, and the bank on the corner of the shopping centre entrance was originally the Kings Arms. Beer was also sometimes brewed in private houses and sold from the front door.

Walk on to Ball Street.

Across the road stands the Golden Ball, one of Poulton's three coaching inns. In the early nineteenth century the pub served as the town's reading room where copies of national newspapers from Manchester, Liverpool and Preston were available. Petty session courts were also held here. Look

Walking Tour

Before the auction mart livestock were sold in the streets.

through the archway – this was the entrance to the stabling at the back. Now simply a car park for the neighbouring supermarket, up to 1968 this was the site of Poulton auction mart with stock being brought here by road from the neighbouring villages and via rail from Ireland. Sales were held two or three times a week. Before the auction mart was opened sales of livestock took place in the streets.

Look across the road to the right.

The property next to the Golden Ball once consisted of two fine houses – the front entrance to one is still in existence serving as a shop doorway. In the mid-nineteenth century one was a small private school with over thirty children boarding there during term time from all over Lancashire.

A ring for tethering animals in the auction mart can still be seen.

The tithe barn.

Next to the supermarket is collection of small early nineteenth cottages, now all shops. Until 1912 when they were demolished, shippons (cowsheds) and workshops lined Ball Street and Church Street backing onto the churchyard from the Thatched House to the church gates in the Market Place.

Stand outside the Golden Ball and look to your right.

This is Tithebarn Street and the front of the car park across the road is the site of the tithe barn, demolished in 1968. The tithe system was introduced into Britain in the eighth century and early tithe barns were built close to the church as this one was, to hold the tithe or one tenth of local produce paid in goods by the inhabitants towards the upkeep of the church and clergy. The system continued in Poulton in some form until the 1930s. In the nineteenth century this tithe barn was used to stage plays and just before its demolition it held workshops run by local craftsmen.

The Breck in the 1920s.

Look further to the right.

In the distance can be seen the original building of the independent chapel erected in 1808 and restored in 1886. The new larger red-brick church beside it dates from 1898; the old chapel now serves as the church hall. Next to it on Queensway can be seen Poulton Methodist church built in 1965 to replace one in Chapel Street.

Walking Tour

The pub at the gate gave welcome refreshments to churchgoers in the past.

Continue to the corner of Ball Street and the Breck.

The large white building on the left was, in 1803, the birthplace of the Revd William Thornber, a noted local historian, an interest he gained from his mother Elizabeth Harrison, who came from an old Fylde family. In 1837 his book *The History of Blackpool* was printed on a hand press in Smith's shop in the Market Place. William became vicar of St John's parish church in Blackpool where he is buried. His parents, Giles and Elizabeth, are buried in a table tomb on the north east corner of St Chad's churchyard.

Take a short walk down the Breck to the railway station.

This was Poulton's second station and was built in 1894. It catered for holiday trains on their way to Blackpool and so has long platforms. Note the emblem of the Lancashire and Yorkshire Railway next to the main door. The first line opened in 1840 and ran from Preston to the new town of Fleetwood, across the bottom of the Breck. When the new station was built the old one became a goods station of which very little now remains.

Look down the Breck.

Breck is a Norse word meaning a slope. Notice the large Victorian houses built in the late nineteenth century by wealthy businessmen who came to

live in Poulton from all over Lancashire. A back street runs behind the houses on the left and the outbuildings, now used as garages, were originally stables.

Walk back towards the church.

The buildings on the left running from the railway bridge to the corner once included a smithy, workshops, cottages and shops all, until 1910, small thatched properties. On the corner of the Breck and Vicarage Road is a building which began as the Ship Inn, became the Working Men's Club and later the Conservative Club. The image of a sailing ship is set into the brickwork high on the front and side walls. Look across Vicarage Road to a fine detached house on the corner. This was the Poulton Savings bank built in 1839. By the end of the nineteenth century it was also in use as a lending library.

The Thatched House pub was erected in 1910 and replaced an ancient cruck-built one that stood at right angles to the present building with its door next to the church gates. Because church-goers often had long distances to travel to attend church, inns were sometimes built next to the church gates. It is possible that this was once known as The Green Man.

The brick wall in Potts Alley was part of the houses that once stood here.

Walk down Chapel Street and into Potts Alley and stop at the small brick wall alongside the churchyard.

Walking Tour

Pause at the entrance to Chapel Street Court and look into the distance where the brick wall on the right curves to the left. This marks the boundary wall of five houses that backed on to the churchyard. In a report of 1848 it was recorded that the inhabitants emptied their chamber pots out of their back bedroom windows 'to the detriment of public health and the gravestones'. There was an open drain running down the middle of Potts Alley as this passageway was known and rats could be seen running across it. Walk down to the curve in the brick wall where two front door steps have been built into the wall. The property opposite was once a lodging house.

Bull Street.

Walk on into the Market Place turn to the left and walk towards the market cross.

Next to the cross are the whipping post, the fish slab and stocks. It is rare to find such a collection of items preserved together. The whipping post and stocks were used to punish wrongdoers and the poor well into the eighteenth century. The flat slab was used for the sale of fish, and lodging house-keepers from the growing bathing resort of Blackpool came to Poulton to buy fresh produce. The painted strips on the west side properties were added in the late nineteenth century.

The corner of Chapel Street and Queens Square.

Look across the road facing the stocks to the Bull.

Walking Tour

The Bull was once one of Poulton's three coaching inns and was rebuilt in the 1950s. Next to it, now a bank, is the site of Alexander Rigby's town house where the family would spend the winter in more congenial surroundings than their main home Layton Hall near Blackpool. Next to the bank is a three-storey house built of hand-made Georgian brick. It was the home of James Baines, a woollen merchant from Goosnargh. From his window he would have been able to see wrong-doers and beggars being punished in the stocks and this may have had something to do with his decision to leave money in his will, when he died in 1717, for three free schools for poor boys. All are still in existence and bear his name – two primary schools in Thornton and Marton and a secondary school in Poulton. He also left money for apprenticeships. A wealthy man, he lent money to local people before the time of banks and building societies. From this point look back at the church for a good view of the Market Place.

Turn left into Queens Square.

On the left is a frieze illustrating the seasons. Below was once the entrance to the stables of a coaching inn – the Spread Eagle. Stand back from the building and the three-storey, double-fronted shape of the inn is clearly still visible. In the late nineteenth century there was a jam factory and corn mill at the back of these buildings and a café, offices, meeting room and registrar's office above the shops. Turn to face Hardhorn Road. The fine building opposite was the home of the Viener family in the late nineteenth century. The Miss Veiners were founders of Guiding and

Pupils of Sheaf Street Church of England School in the early 1900s.

Walking Tour

Scouting in Poulton and one became Head of the Church of England school. The building on the left corner was Poulton Institute built in the early 1900s providing facilities for billiards and cards and classes. However it was not well supported and in the 1930s was refitted as Poulton Library. In 1965 a new library was built in Blackpool Old Road and since then the Institute has housed a variety of businesses.

> **Cross Queen's Square and walk a little way down Hardhorn Road.**

On the left is a row of small cottages, one of which was a bakery in the early nineteenth century supplying bread for the Eucharist at St Chad's. Opposite was the home of Samuel Lomas a well known clockmaker who was often called upon to repair the church clock. His clocks are now worth a good deal as collector's items. Further down Hardhorn Road on the left is St Chad's Church of England School, first opened as a Sunday school in 1836, then used as a day school from 1868.

The Market Place in the 1940s.

> **Walk back into Queen's Square.**

The bulge in the footpath marks the original site of the war memorial erected in 1922. It is now in the Market Place. Walk a little further to the corner of Chapel Street on the left. This corner was the site of the first Wesleyan Chapel in Poulton built in 1819. It was replaced by the present shops in 1965 and a new Methodist church opened on Queensway. On

*St Chad's in early
spring.*

the opposite corner is a row of nineteenth-century cottages. In the 1930s the corner property was a shop. On one occasion a bus taking school children on a trip ran into the shop front when one child took the hand brake off! In the distance down Higher Green and Lower Green is a park that now occupies the land that once belonged to St Chad's, known as glebe land. In the early nineteenth century the whole area including Queens Square down to the end of Lower Green was know simply as 'The Green' probably marking the medieval town green.

Walk up Chapel Street to St Chad's churchyard and take the diagonal path through the churchyard to the church.

In the Spring the ground is covered with a sequence of snowdrops, crocuses and daffodils. The earliest record of a church here is 1094 but it is likely that there was a Saxon church already here. Although the present building has a typical Georgian exterior the grey ashlar stone is only a thin skin placed in 1751 on top of the original red sandstone building material. The tower dates from the mid-seventeenth century and the apse from 1868. Inside are the original eighteenth-century galleries, some still retaining their box pews and name plates. A guide book giving more details is available in the church. The church is open every day during daylight hours and is well worth a visit to complete this walking tour of Poulton-le-Fylde.

Index